OLD

HOR
AND ASTRAL
DIARY

CAPRICORN

OLD MOORE'S

HOROSCOPE AND ASTRAL DIARY

♑

CAPRICORN

foulsham
LONDON • NEW YORK • TORONTO • SYDNEY

foulsham
Capital Point, 33 Bath Road, Slough, Berkshire, SL1 3UF, England

Foulsham books can be found in all good bookshops and direct from
www.foulsham.com

ISBN: 978-0-572-03661-4

A CIP record for this book is available from the British Library

Printed in Great Britain by Cox & Wyman Ltd, Reading, Berkshire.

CONTENTS

INTRODUCTION

Astrology has been with us for a very long time and our fascination for the starry heavens seems to go back many thousands of years. Incised bones carrying lunar calendars have been found that are tens of thousands of years old, and our belief that the stars and planets have a bearing on our daily lives could easily be almost as ancient. Astrology was studied in all the major civilisations, and shows no signs of diminishing in popularity in the 21st century. Old Moore, a time-served veteran in astrological research, continues to monitor the zodiac and has produced the Astral Diary for 2012, tailor-made to your own astrological make-up.

Old Moore's Astral Diary is unique in its ability to get the heart of your nature and to offer you the sort of advice that might come from a trusted friend. The Diaries are structured in such a way that you can see in a day-by-day sense exactly how the planets are working for you. The diary section advises how you can get the best from upcoming situations and allows you to plan ahead successfully. There is room in the daily sections to put your own observations or even appointments, and the book is conveniently structured to stay with you throughout the year.

Whilst other popular astrology books merely deal with your astrological Sun sign, the Astral Diaries go much further. Every person on the planet is unique, and Old Moore allows you to access your individuality in a number of ways. The front section gives you the chance to work out the placement of the Moon at the time of your birth and to see how its position has set an important seal on your overall nature. Perhaps most important of all, you can use the Astral Diary to discover your Rising sign. This is the zodiac sign that was appearing over the Eastern horizon at the time of your birth, and is just as important to you as an individual as is your Sun sign.

It is the synthesis of many different astrological possibilities that makes you what you are, and with the Astral Diaries you can learn so much. How do you react to love and romance? Through the unique Venus tables and the readings that follow them, you can learn where the planet Venus was at the time of your birth. It is even possible to register when little Mercury is 'retrograde', which means that it appears to be moving backwards in space when viewed from the Earth. Mercury rules communication, so be prepared to deal with a few setbacks in this area when you see the sign ☿. The Astral Diary will be an interest and a support throughout the whole year ahead.

Old Moore extends his customary greeting to all people of the Earth and offers his age-old wishes for a happy and prosperous period ahead.

THE ESSENCE OF CAPRICORN

Exploring the Personality of Capricorn the Goat

(22nd DECEMBER – 20th JANUARY)

What's in a sign?

You probably think of yourself as being the least complicated person to be found anywhere. Although this is basically true, that doesn't necessarily mean that everyone understands you quite as well as they might. When faced with the real world you are practical, capable and resourceful. That means that you get on well with whatever needs to be done. Where you might sometimes fall down is in terms of communicating your intentions to the world at large – mostly it doesn't seem all that important to do so. In other words, you are not the world's best talker, and probably don't even want to be.

When it comes to sweeping away the red tape and actually getting down to the task in hand, you are second to none. Dextrous and adaptable in all matters that need your unique logic, you come at all problems with the same determination to sort them out. However, your ruling planet is cold, ponderous Saturn, and that could be where the potential problems start. Although you have a kind heart and a genuine desire to improve the lot of others, your methods are sometimes misunderstood. Some people might think you a little aloof, or even difficult to talk to. You have frequent quiet spells and often seem to be particularly content with your own company. On rare occasions this can leave you isolated.

Sharing what you are with the world at large is the most important factor on the road to a more contented life, though even this isn't certain, because most Capricorn people tend to be fairly happy with being the way they are. All the same, when those around you want to see something actually being done, they will call on you. Success is not hard for you to achieve, particularly in a career sense. You don't mind getting your hands dirty and can usually be relied upon to find ingenious answers when they are most needed.

In matters of love you are sincere and will work long and hard for your family. Romantically speaking you take some time to get going but can be ardent and sincere when you finally do. Routines don't bother you, and you can also learn to be adaptable.

Capricorn resources

You probably don't think of yourself as being the most dynamic person in the world, though you certainly are one of the most capable. When others are looking for answers, even in very practical matters, you are in there sorting things out. It's the nuts and bolts of the world that are most important, and you don't seem to have too much trouble fixing broken things – whether it's the living room chair, or the heart of a dear friend. Instead of trying to be one of life's exciting go-getters, you are likely to be more comfortable working slowly and steadily, sometimes in the background. But this doesn't mean that you fail to make a positive impression. On the contrary, you are very necessary to those who form a part of your life, and they are ever aware of the important part you play. It isn't given to everyone to be showy and flashy, and in any case even if you forced yourself down such roads you probably wouldn't be at all comfortable in a role that doesn't come naturally to you.

One of your greatest attributes is your dry sense of humour. It's always possible for you to make others laugh, even during the most awkward or difficult situations. When the world looks particularly dark we all need a Capricorn subject along to lighten the load. You make a good colleague, know well how to co-operate and tend to work capably, either as part of a team, or when circumstances dictate, on your own.

Your greatest resource, and the one that has made many Capricorn people famous over the years, is your capacity to keep going. When there is a problem to be solved, a bridge to build, or a family to support under difficult circumstances, you really come into your own. This is probably because you don't understand the meaning of the word failure. You can find ways round any number of obstacles, and remain dependable, even when the world and his dog are falling to pieces. Add to this the fact that you are consistent and reliable and it shouldn't be too hard for you to enjoy being a capable Capricorn.

Beneath the surface

Although you might not appear to be very complicated when viewed from the perspective of those who see you on a daily basis, you are actually very complex. The reason that this is not obvious lies in the fact that you betray very little of your inner mind in your day-to-day interactions with others. In the main they see you as being capable and settled – but how wrong they can be.

The fact is that you are rarely totally sure of yourself. The confidence to get things done disguises how often you shake inside, and especially so if you are forced into the public arena. You probably wouldn't relish having to do any sort of presentation or to be put on the spot in front of individuals you consider to be more dynamic than you are. Despite this there are strong saving graces. Even when times are tough, or when you do feel a little shaky inside, your natural way forward is to keep plugging away. In some respects your zodiac sign may represent one of the bravest of them all. You won't allow yourself to be bettered by anyone, and the more pressure that is put upon you to fail, the greater is your internal desire for success.

In matters of emotion you are complicated and difficult to understand. You view relationships with the same patience that you bring to almost all facets of life. Friends can misuse or even abuse you for a while, but there is a breaking point within Capricorn that appears sudden, and very final. And once you have made up your mind to a particular course of action, there isn't any force in the world that will prevent you from implementing it.

Your natural planetary ruler is Saturn, the Lord of Time. As a result you are inclined to see things in the medium and longer term. You rarely show yourself to be impatient and carefully choose a course of action, using mental processes that usually follow tried and tested paths. You won't be hurried or pushed and will always stick to methods of working that seem to have worked for you in the past. Although this might sometimes make you feel lacking in colour or variety, you almost always get where you want to go. Occasionally your inner mind takes a great leap in logic. This can lead to a sudden change in attitude and actions that will shock the world. And why not? Even Capricorns need to keep people guessing sometimes.

You may not be the easiest person in the world to understand, or to get to know fully. Don't worry. The inner secrecy of your nature is half your appeal.

Making the best of yourself

We all need to realise what makes us tick, and to come to terms with the most comfortable way in which we can react with the world at large. This is just as true for the zodiac sign of Capricorn as it is for any other. But nobody is perfect, so what can you do to use your skills to the full and to get on better with those who share the planet with you?

Well for starters, it wouldn't be a bad idea to let others know what you are doing – and why. In practical situations especially it's sometimes much easier for you simply to get on and finish a task on your own. And despite your capabilities this is probably why you are not the world's best teacher. It's simply less complicated to get something done, and then to move on patiently to the next demand. On the way, however, you might alienate those who would love to be your friends, and to learn from you.

When it comes to emotion you should do your best to explain the way you feel. Building up animosity for days, weeks or even months, doesn't really do anyone a lot of good, not even a Capricorn subject. People can't alter to suit your needs if they don't know what it is you want. For this reason you should always be as honest as you can be, even if this proves to be quite embarrassing at first. Be willing to show your flexible side – and even to create one if necessary. Try doing things the way others want to proceed now and again, despite the fact that you could be convinced that they are wrong in their approach. Allowing those around you the right to fail is important and in the end it will only make you look that much more confident and together when you stoop to pick up the pieces.

As often as proves to be possible you should display the inner smile that burns away inside you. Be willing to let your hair down and have a good time in the company of people who really do want to know that you are happy. Most important of all, share your inner honesty with those who are important to you.

The impressions you give

There is a great disparity between the way you feel about certain situations, and the impression you offer to an unsuspecting world. If you could fully see yourself as others usually see you, it's an odds-on certainty that you would be very surprised. The vast majority of those with whom you live and work see you as being ultra confident, very cool and quite capable. If you find this hard to believe, simply ask the most honest of your friends. It doesn't matter how you feel inside, or that you often have to dig around for answers that don't supply themselves immediately. What counts is the barrier that is placed constantly between your inner mind and your outward persona.

This is very important because it means you could get on in life even better than you may appear to be doing at the moment. Think what a great gift it is rarely to show that you are quaking inside. And when your cool approach means that you find advancement coming your way, you move on to the next set of requirements with the same apparent confidence you had before.

On a less positive note, it is possible that certain of the people with whom you interact on a daily basis could find you somewhat cold and even perhaps a little aloof on occasions. This is not the case, but once again there is a screen between the way you feel and the façade you show to the world at large. And though this barrier can be your best friend, it can also be a powerful enemy, especially in emotional or romantic situations. When circumstances necessitate, it is important that you tell those with whom you share your life exactly how you feel. That allows them to modify their own behaviour to suit your needs.

There may not be a great deal of work to do on altering your approach because in the main you are well liked and certainly respected. All that is really required in any case is an understanding that what you think and the way you act are not necessarily the same thing.

The way forward

Although it's true of course that anyone can make favourable alterations to their life, it's entirely possible that yours is already headed in the right direction generally. Capricorn people are not usually too complicated; they remain modest in their objectives and can achieve their ends through the medium of good ideas and hard work. You may not give the impression of being the most exciting person in the world – and nor do you wish to be. But when it's necessary to come up with the goods, mentally and practically, you don't usually have much trouble doing so.

To be and to remain quietly confident isn't too much to ask from life. Under most circumstances you take on tasks that you know you can achieve, try to be kind to others on the way and don't tend to make too many waves. It probably doesn't bother you too much that there are people around who may not care for you. This is essentially because you are a realist and understand that you won't be everyone's cup of tea.

If there are points within your nature that could be improved with effort they might relate to a certain stubborn streak. There are occasions when you become very determined to achieve a particular objective and you may not always listen to alternatives once you think you know how to proceed. However, since you don't tend to take on tasks that you are not equipped to deal with, what some may call intransigence, you might refer to as self-assurance. It is also possible that you sometimes find it difficult to express your inner feelings, and especially those related to love. You can be somewhat suspicious of the motives of others and may guard yourself a little too carefully as a result.

Try to recognise that there is more than one way to skin a cat, and that you can actually learn and grow through co-operation. You may also need to be willing to take on a greater degree of responsibility at work, even though this might go against the grain for a whole host of reasons. When faced with decisions that have a bearing on the lives of others, seek their counsel and take note of their opinions.

There are times when you can be a little too pessimistic for your own good. It is important to cultivate a cheerful approach, even though your sometimes slightly gloomy attitude is actually revered and smiled at by your friends. You are loyal, hard-working and generally kind. Capricorn may not be the most dynamic of the zodiac signs, but it is hard to fault it all the same.

CAPRICORN ON THE CUSP

Old Moore is often asked how astrological profiles are altered for those people born at either the beginning or the end of a zodiac sign, or, more properly, on the cusps of a sign. In the case of Capricorn this would be on the 22nd of December and for two or three days after, and similarly at the end of the sign, probably from the 18th to the 20th of January. In this year's Astral Diaries, once again, Old Moore sets out to explain the differences regarding cuspid signs.

The Sagittarius Cusp – December 22nd to 24th

Oh, what a lovely person you can be, and how respected you are by the world at large. At its best this is a very fortunate combination because it retains all the practical skills of Capricorn, but the nature is somewhat elevated by the quality of Sagittarius. Nothing much is beyond your capabilities but, unlike the typical Sagittarian, you back up your words with some quite practical actions. People learn to trust you and the amount of reliance that is placed on your judgement is sometimes staggering. Of course this does infer a high degree of responsibility but this fact probably won't worry you in the slightest. From a personal point of view you are very good to know and do your best to be friendly to almost everyone. However, you don't suffer fools at all gladly and probably prefer the company of those whose thoughts and ideas run along the same sort of road as yours.

Nobody could dispute the fact that you are very reasonable but you do sometimes get so obsessed with things that you could be less accessible than Sagittarius. A little extra work may be needed in this direction, especially when you are dealing with people who don't have your fast-track approach to problems. For all this you are a deep thinker and will often weigh up the pros and cons of a particular problem if necessary. In love you are deep and sincere, but with a superficial veneer that makes you appear light, bright and fun to be with. Making your way in life isn't at all difficult and money could easily come your way. This is not a response to good luck, but to dedication and inspired hard work.

With a good combination of the practical and the inspirational, you could turn your hand to almost anything. Your confidence is usually high and you are always in a good position to get by, no matter what obstacles you encounter. You like a challenge and rarely shy away from things when the going gets tough. This is one of the reasons that others like you so much and also explains why they have such confidence in your abilities. Your sense of purpose is strong and you may be tougher than you realise.

The Aquarius Cusp – January 18th to 20th

This is the more dreamy side of Capricorn and can make for an individual who is sometimes rather difficult for others to fathom. This is hardly surprising since you don't really know your own nature quite as well as you would wish. Because the two zodiac signs are a little like oil and water you can rub along quite nicely for ages as a typical Capricorn, before suddenly shooting off at a tangent into some nether world that isn't at all like the reliable sign of the Goat. You tend to think about things fairly deeply, though with a rather 'off the wall' approach that sometimes annoys your deeper Capricorn traits. Certainly you are fascinating to know, with a magnetic personality and a basic charm that shows itself a great deal, especially when your interest is roused.

You are a lover of mystery and might appear on occasion to have a slightly dark side. This is really only a sort of morbid curiosity and it doesn't reflect your own basic nature, which is kind, sincere and anxious to please. Socially you contribute to anything that takes your fancy but you won't stay around long if you find a conversation boring. Finding the right sort of romantic partner might be somewhat difficult because you are not run-of-the-mill and have strange needs at a personal level. However, once you have set your sights in a particular direction, you stick to it. And as far as finding the right person is concerned, you could do much worse than to trust your intuition, which is strong. You don't always know what you want from life, but this fact can prove to be half of the fascination.

This unusual nature tends to fit you for occupations that demand a variety of skills, though you may change your career entirely at some stage in your life. Certainly you can be very practical, but the way things feel is important to you and you might find that you start certain tasks time and again in order to make sure that they turn out just right. This sign combination can easily lead to a desire for travel and a need to extend your personal horizons. Your restlessness is sometimes a puzzle to others, but it's a fascination, too.

CAPRICORN AND ITS ASCENDANTS

The nature of every individual on the planet is composed of the rich variety of zodiac signs and planetary positions that were present at the time of their birth. Your Sun sign, which in your case is Capricorn, is one of the many factors when it comes to assessing the unique person you are. Probably the most important consideration, other than your Sun sign, is to establish the zodiac sign that was rising over the eastern horizon at the time that you were born. This is your Ascending or Rising sign. Most popular astrology fails to take account of the Ascendant, and yet its importance remains with you from the very moment of your birth, through every day of your life. The Ascendant is evident in the way you approach the world, and so, when meeting a person for the first time, it is this astrological influence that you are most likely to notice first. Our Ascending sign essentially represents what we appear to be, while the Sun sign is what we feel inside ourselves.

The Ascendant also has the potential for modifying our overall nature. For example, if you were born at a time of day when Capricorn was passing over the eastern horizon (this would be around the time of dawn) then you would be classed as a double Capricorn. As such, you would typify this zodiac sign, both internally and in your dealings with others. However, if your Ascendant sign turned out to be an Air sign, such as Gemini, there would be a profound alteration of nature, away from the expected qualities of Capricorn.

One of the reasons why popular astrology often ignores the Ascendant is that it has always been rather difficult to establish. Old Moore has found a way to make this possible by devising an easy-to-use table, which you will find on page 159 of this book. Using this, you can establish your Ascendant sign at a glance. You will need to know your rough time of birth, then it is simply a case of following the instructions.

For those readers who have no idea of their time of birth it might be worth allowing a good friend, or perhaps your partner, to read through the section that follows this introduction. Someone who deals with you on a regular basis may easily discover your Ascending sign, even though you could have some difficulty establishing it for yourself. A good understanding of this component of your nature is essential if you want to be aware of that 'other person' who is responsible for the way you make contact with the world at large. Your Sun sign, Ascendant sign, and the other pointers in this book will, together, allow you a far better understanding of what makes you tick as an individual. Peeling back the different layers of your astrological make-up can be an enlightening experience, and the Ascendant may represent one of the most important layers of all.

Capricorn with Capricorn Ascendant

Whatever it is that you are looking for in life, there isn't much doubt that you find it. Having done so, you tend to consolidate your position before looking ahead to the next set of objectives. There isn't a more determined soul than you in the length and breadth of the whole zodiac and you will not be thwarted once you have made up your mind. It would take an astute person to pull the wool over your eyes in any practical respect, though you may not be quite so clever when it comes to the personal side of your life. You can sometimes be rather misled in love, but not if you are as determined in this direction as you are in every other sphere of life.

The most enduring quality that you possess is staying-power, and you remain certain that your long-term plans are the right ones, modifying here and tweaking there to get them just right. On the way you make few deep friends, though the ones you do have tend to stay around for years. All the same you are popular, and can attract the right sort of people to help you out. In love you are sincere and honest, a good and reliable partner, and, I am told, one of the best lovers to be found in a month of Sundays. All you need to complete the picture is a more flexible attitude.

Capricorn with Aquarius Ascendant

Here the determination of Capricorn is assisted by a slightly more adaptable quality and an off-beat personality that tends to keep everyone else guessing. You don't care to be quite so predictable as the archetypal Capricorn would be and there is a more idealistic quality, or at least one that shows more. A greater number of friends than Capricorn would usually keep is likely, though less than a true Aquarian would gather. Few people doubt your sincerity, though not all of them understand what makes you tick. Unfortunately you are not in a position to help them out, because you are not very sure yourself. All the same you muddle through and can be very capable when the mood takes you.

Being a natural traveller, you love to see new places and would be quite fascinated by cultures that are very different to your own. People with this combination are inclined to spend some time living abroad and may even settle there. You look out for the underdog and will always have time for a good cause, no matter what it takes to help. In romantic terms you are a reliable partner, though with a slightly wayward edge which, if anything, tends to make you more attractive. Listen to your intuition, which rarely lets you down. Generally speaking you are very popular.

Capricorn with Pisces Ascendant

You are certainly not the easiest person in the world to understand, mainly because your nature is so deep and your personality so complicated, that others are somewhat intimidated at the prospect of staring into this abyss. All the same your friendly nature is attractive, and there will always be people around who are fascinated by the sheer magnetic quality that is endemic to the zodiac mix. Sentimental and extremely kind, there is no limit to the extent of your efforts on behalf of a deserving world, though there are some people around who wonder at your commitment and who may ridicule you a little for your staying-power, even in the face of some adversity. At work you are very capable, will work long and hard, and can definitely expect a greater degree of financial and practical success than Pisces alone. Routines don't bother you too much, though you do need regular periods of introspection, which help to recharge low batteries and a battered self-esteem.

In affairs of the heart you are somewhat given to impulse, which belies the more careful qualities of Capricorn. However, the determination remains intact and you are quite capable of chasing rainbows around, never realising that you can't get to the end of them. You are immensely lovable and a great favourite to many.

Capricorn with Aries Ascendant

If ever anyone could be accused of setting off immediately, but slowly, it has to be you. These are very contradictory signs and the differences will express themselves in a variety of ways. One thing is certain, you have tremendous tenacity and will see a job through patiently from beginning to end, without tiring on the way, and ensuring that every detail is taken care of properly. This combination often bestows good health and a great capacity for continuity, particularly in terms of the length of life. You are certainly not as argumentative as the typical Aries, but you do know how to get your own way, which is just as well because you are usually thinking on behalf of everyone else and not just on your own account.

At home you can relax, which is a blessing for Aries, though in fact you seldom choose to do so because you always have some project or other on the go. You probably enjoy knocking down and rebuilding walls, though this is a practical tendency and not responsive to relationships, in which you are ardent and sincere. Impetuosity is as close to your heart as is the case for any type of Aries subject, though you certainly have the ability to appear patient and steady. But it's really just a front, isn't it?

Capricorn with Taurus Ascendant

It might appear on the surface that you are not the most interesting person in the world. This is a pity, for you have an active though very logical mind, so logical in some instances that you would have a great deal in common with Mr Spock. This is the thorn in your flesh, or rather the flesh of everyone else, since you are probably quite happy being exactly what you are. You can think things through in a clear and very practical way and end up taking decisions that are balanced, eminently sensible, but, on occasions, rather dull.

Actually there is a fun machine somewhere deep within that Earth-sign nature and those who know you the best will recognise the fact. Often this combination is attended by a deep and biting sense of humour, but it's of the sort that less intelligent and considered types would find rather difficult to recognise. It is likely that you have no lack of confidence in your own judgement, and you have all the attributes necessary to do very well on the financial front. Slow and steady progress is your way and you need to be quite certain before you commit yourself to any new venture. This is a zodiac combination that can soak up years of stress and numerous difficulties and yet still come out on top. Nothing holds you back for long and you tend to be very brave.

Capricorn with Gemini Ascendant

A very careful and considered combination is evident here. You still have the friendly and chatty qualities of Gemini, though you also possess an astute, clever and deep-thinking quality which can really add bite to the Mercurial aspects of your nature. Although you rarely seem to take yourself or anyone else too seriously, in reality you are not easily fooled and usually know the direction in which you are heading. The practical application of your thought processes matter to you and you always give of your best, especially in any professional situation. This combination provides the very best business mind that any Gemini could have and, unlike other versions of the sign, you are willing to allow matters to mature. This quality cannot be overstated and leads to a form of ultimate achievement that many other Geminis would only guess at.

Family matters are important to you and your home is a special place of retreat, even though you are also willing to get out and meet the world, which is the prerogative of all Gemini types. There are times when you genuinely wish to remain quiet, and when such times arise you may need to explain the situation to some of the bemused people surrounding you. Above all you look towards material gain, though without ever losing your sense of humour.

Capricorn with Cancer Ascendant

The single most important factor here is the practical ability to get things done and to see any task, professional or personal, through to the end. Since half this combination is Cancer that also means expounding much of your energy on behalf of others. There isn't a charity in the world that would fail to recognise what a potent combination this is when it comes to the very concrete side of offering help and assistance. Many of your ideas hold water and you don't set off on abortive journeys of any kind, simply because you tend to get the ground rules fixed in your mind first.

On a more personal level you can be rather hard to get to know, because both these signs have a deep quality and a tendency to keep things in the dark. The mystery may only serve to encourage people to try and get to know you better. As a result you could attract a host of admirers, many of whom would wish to form romantic attachments. This may prove to be irrelevant however, because once you give your heart, you tend to be loyal and would only change your mind if you were pushed into doing so. Prolonged periods of inactivity don't do you any good and it is sensible for you to keep on the move, even though your progress in life is measured and very steady.

Capricorn with Leo Ascendant

What really sets you apart is your endless patience and your determination to get where you want to go, no matter how long it takes you to do so. On the way there are many sub-plots in your life and a wealth of entertaining situations to keep you amused. Probably somewhat quieter than the average Leo, you still have the capacity to be the life and soul of the party on those occasions when it suits you to be so. Energy, when allied to persistence, is a powerful commodity and you have a great need to take on causes of one sort or another. Probably at your best when defending the rights of the oppressed, you take the protecting qualities of Leo to greater heights than almost anyone else touched by the idealistic and regal qualities of the sign. If arguments come into your life, you deal with them quickly and, in the main, wisely. Like most Capricorn types you take to a few individuals, who will play a part in your life for years on end.

Being a good family type, your partner and children are very important and you will lavish the same patience, determination and ultimate success on their behalf that you do when dealing with more remote situations. The fact is that you do not know any other way to behave, and you are at your best when there is a mountain to climb.

Capricorn with Virgo Ascendant

Your endurance, persistence and concentration are legendary, and there is virtually nothing that eludes you once you have the bit between your teeth. You are not the pushy, fussy, go-getting sort of Virgoan but are steady, methodical and very careful. Once you have made up your mind, a whole team of wild horses could not change it, and although this can be a distinct blessing at times, it is a quality that can bring odd problems into your life too. The difficulty starts when you adopt a lost or less than sensible cause. Even in the face of overwhelming negative evidence, there is something inside you that prevents any sort of U-turn and so you carry on as solidly as only you can, to a destination that won't suit you at all.

There are few people around who are more loyal and constant than you can be. There is a lighter and brighter side to your nature, and the one or two people who are most important in your life will know how to bring it out. You have a wicked sense of humour, particularly if you have had a drink or when you are feeling on top form. Travel does you the world of good, even if there is a part of you that would rather stay at home. You have a potent, powerful and magnetic personality, but for much of the time it is kept carefully hidden.

Capricorn with Libra Ascendant

It is a fact that Libra is the most patient of the Air signs, though like the others it needs to get things done fairly quickly. Capricorn, on the other hand, will work long and hard to achieve its objectives and will not be thwarted. As a result this is a powerful combination and one that leads ultimately to success.

Capricorn is often accused of taking itself too seriously, and yet it has an ironic and really very funny sense of humour which only its chief confidants recognise. Libra is lighthearted, always willing to have fun and quite anxious to please. When these two basic types come together in their best forms, you might find yourself to be one of the most well-balanced people around. Certainly you know what you want, but don't have to use a bulldozer in order to get it.

Active and enthusiastic when something really takes your fancy, you might also turn out to be one of the very best lovers of them all. The reason for this is that you have the depth of Capricorn but the lighter and more directly affectionate qualities of the Scales. What you want from life in a personal sense, you eventually tend to get, but you don't care too much if this takes you a while. Few people could deny that you are a faithful friend, a happy sort and a deeply magnetic personality.

Capricorn with Scorpio Ascendant

If patience, perseverance and a solid ability to get where you want to go are considered to be the chief components of a happy life, then you should be skipping about every day. Unfortunately this is not always the case, and here we have two zodiac signs who can both be too deep for their own good. Both Scorpio and Capricorn are inclined to take themselves rather too seriously, and your main lesson in life, and some would say the reason you have adopted this zodiac combination, is to 'lighten up'. If all that determination is pushed in the direction of your service to the world at large, you are seen as being one of the kindest people imaginable. This is really the only option for you, because if you turn this tremendous potential power inwards all the time you will become brooding, secretive and sometimes even selfish. Your eyes should be turned towards a needy humanity, which can be served with the dry but definite wit of Capricorn and the true compassion of Scorpio.

It is impossible with this combination to indicate what areas of life suit you the best. Certainly you adore luxury in all its forms, and yet you can get by with almost nothing. You desire travel, and at the same time love the comforts and stability of home. The people who know you best are aware that you are rather special. Listen to what they say.

Capricorn with Sagittarius Ascendant

The typical Sagittarian nature is modified for the better when Capricorn is part of the deal. It's true that you manage to push forward progressively under most circumstances, but you also possess staying power and can work long and hard to achieve your objectives, most of which are carefully planned in advance. Few people have the true measure of your nature, for it runs rather deeper than appears to be the case on the surface. Routines don't bother you as much as would be the case for Sagittarius when taken alone, and you don't care if any objective takes weeks, months or even years to achieve. You are very fond of those you take to and would certainly prove to be a capable friend, even when things get quite tough.

In love relationships you are steadfast and reliable, and yet you never lose the ability to entertain. Yours is a dry sense of humour which shows itself to a multitude of different people and which doesn't run out, even on those occasions when life gets tough. It might take you a long time to find the love of your life, but when you do there is a greater possibility of retaining the relationship for a long period. You don't tend to inherit money, but you can easily make it for yourself, though you won't worry too much about the amount. On the whole you are a very self-sufficient and sensible individual.

THE MOON AND THE PART IT PLAYS IN YOUR LIFE

In astrology the Moon is probably the single most important heavenly body after the Sun. Its unique position, as partner to the Earth on its journey around the solar system, means that the Moon appears to pass through the signs of the zodiac extremely quickly. The zodiac position of the Moon at the time of your birth plays a great part in personal character and is especially significant in the build-up of your emotional nature.

Sun Moon Cycles

The first lunar cycle deals with the part the position of the Moon plays relative to your Sun sign. I have made the fluctuations of this pattern easy for you to understand by means of a simple cyclic graph. It appears on the first page of each 'Your Month At A Glance', under the title 'Highs and Lows'. The graph displays the lunar cycle and you will soon learn to understand how its movements have a bearing on your level of energy and your abilities.

Your Own Moon Sign

Discovering the position of the Moon at the time of your birth has always been notoriously difficult because tracking the complex zodiac positions of the Moon is not easy. This process has been reduced to three simple stages with Old Moore's unique Lunar Tables. A breakdown of the Moon's zodiac positions can be found from page 25 onwards, so that once you know what your Moon Sign is, you can see what part this plays in the overall build-up of your personal character.

If you follow the instructions on the next page you will soon be able to work out exactly what zodiac sign the Moon occupied on the day that you were born and you can then go on to compare the reading for this position with those of your Sun sign and your Ascendant. It is partly the comparison between these three important positions that goes towards making you the unique individual you are.

HOW TO DISCOVER YOUR MOON SIGN

This is a three-stage process. You may need a pen and a piece of paper but if you follow the instructions below the process should only take a minute or so.

STAGE 1 First of all you need to know the Moon Age at the time of your birth. If you look at Moon Table 1, on page 23, you will find all the years between 1914 and 2012 down the left side. Find the year of your birth and then trace across to the right to the month of your birth. Where the two intersect you will find a number. This is the date of the New Moon in the month that you were born. You now need to count forward the number of days between the New Moon and your own birthday. For example, if the New Moon in the month of your birth was shown as being the 6th and you were born on the 20th, your Moon Age Day would be 14. If the New Moon in the month of your birth came after your birthday, you need to count forward from the New Moon in the previous month. Whatever the result, jot this number down so that you do not forget it.

STAGE 2 Take a look at Moon Table 2 on page 24. Down the left hand column look for the date of your birth. Now trace across to the month of your birth. Where the two meet you will find a letter. Copy this letter down alongside your Moon Age Day.

STAGE 3 Moon Table 3 on page 24 will supply you with the zodiac sign the Moon occupied on the day of your birth. Look for your Moon Age Day down the left hand column and then for the letter you found in Stage 2. Where the two converge you will find a zodiac sign and this is the sign occupied by the Moon on the day that you were born.

Your Zodiac Moon Sign Explained

You will find a profile of all zodiac Moon Signs on pages 25 to 28, showing in yet another way how astrology helps to make you into the individual that you are. In each daily entry of the Astral Diary you can find the zodiac position of the Moon for every day of the year. This also allows you to discover your lunar birthdays. Since the Moon passes through all the signs of the zodiac in about a month, you can expect something like twelve lunar birthdays each year. At these times you are likely to be emotionally steady and able to make the sort of decisions that have real, lasting value.

MOON TABLE 1

YEAR	NOV	DEC	JAN
1914	17	17	25
1915	7	6	15
1916	26	25	5
1917	14	13	24
1918	3	2	12
1919	22	21	1/31
1920	10	10	20
1921	29	29	9
1922	19	18	27
1923	8	8	17
1924	26	26	6
1925	16	15	24
1926	5	5	14
1927	24	24	3
1928	12	12	21
1929	1	1/30	11
1930	20	19	29
1931	9	9	18
1932	27	27	7
1933	17	17	25
1934	7	6	15
1935	26	25	5
1936	14	13	24
1937	3	2	12
1938	22	21	1/31
1939	11	10	20
1940	29	28	9
1941	19	18	27
1942	8	8	16
1943	27	27	6
1944	15	15	25
1945	4	4	14
1946	23	23	3
1947	12	12	21
1948	1	1/30	11
1949	20	19	29
1950	9	9	18
1951	29	28	7
1952	17	17	26
1953	6	6	15
1954	25	25	5
1955	14	14	24
1956	2	2	13
1957	21	21	1/30
1958	11	10	19
1959	30	29	9
1960	19	18	27
1961	8	7	16
1962	27	26	6
1963	15	15	25
1964	4	4	14
1965	22	22	3
1966	12	12	21
1967	2	1/30	10
1968	21	20	29
1969	9	9	19
1970	29	28	7
1971	18	17	26
1972	6	6	15
1973	25	25	5
1974	14	14	24
1975	3	3	12
1976	21	21	1/31
1977	11	10	19
1978	30	29	9
1979	19	18	27
1980	8	7	16
1981	26	26	6
1982	15	15	25
1983	4	4	14
1984	22	22	3
1985	12	12	21
1986	2	1/30	10
1987	21	20	29
1988	9	9	19
1989	28	28	7
1990	17	17	26
1991	6	6	15
1992	24	24	4
1993	14	14	22
1994	3	2	11
1995	22	22	1
1996	11	10	20
1997	30	29	9
1998	19	18	28
1999	8	7	17
2000	27	25	6
2001	16	15	24
2002	4	4	13
2003	24	23	3
2004	11	11	21
2005	1	1	10
2006	20	20	29
2007	9	9	18
2008	28	27	8
2009	17	16	26
2010	6	6	15
2011	25	25	4
2012	13	12	23

TABLE 2

DAY	DEC	JAN
1	i	A
2	i	A
3	m	A
4	m	A
5	n	A
6	n	A
7	n	A
8	n	A
9	n	A
10	n	A
11	n	B
12	n	B
13	n	B
14	n	B
15	n	B
16	n	B
17	n	B
18	n	B
19	n	B
20	n	B
21	n	C
22	n	C
23	q	C
24	q	C
25	q	C
26	q	C
27	q	C
28	q	C
29	q	C
30	q	C
31	q	C

TABLE 3

M/D	i	m	n	q	A	B	C
0	SA	SA	SA	CP	CP	AQ	AQ
1	SA	SA	CP	CP	AQ	AQ	AQ
2	CP	CP	CP	AQ	AQ	AQ	PI
3	CP	CP	AQ	AQ	AQ	PI	PI
4	CP	AQ	AQ	PI	PI	PI	AR
5	AQ	AQ	PI	PI	PI	AR	AR
6	AQ	AQ	PI	AR	AR	AR	AR
7	PI	PI	AR	AR	AR	AR	TA
8	PI	PI	AR	AR	AR	TA	TA
9	AR	AR	TA	TA	TA	TA	GE
10	AR	AR	TA	TA	TA	GE	GE
11	TA	TA	TA	GE	GE	GE	GE
12	TA	TA	GE	GE	GE	GE	CA
13	GE	GE	GE	GE	GE	CA	CA
14	GE	GE	CA	CA	CA	CA	LE
15	GE	GE	GE	CA	CA	LE	LE
16	GE	CA	CA	CA	LE	LE	LE
17	CA	CA	CA	LE	LE	LE	VI
18	CA	CA	LE	LE	LE	VI	VI
19	CA	LE	LE	LE	VI	VI	VI
20	LE	LE	LE	VI	VI	LI	LI
21	LE	LE	VI	VI	LI	LI	LI
22	VI	VI	VI	LI	LI	LI	SC
23	VI	VI	VI	LI	LI	SC	SC
24	VI	VI	LI	LI	SC	SC	SC
25	LI	LI	LI	SC	SC	SA	SA
26	LI	LI	SC	SC	SA	SA	SA
27	SC	SC	SC	SA	SA	SA	CP
28	SC	SC	SC	SA	SA	CP	CP
29	SC	SA	SA	SA	CP	CP	CP

AR = Aries, TA = Taurus, GE = Gemini, CA = Cancer, LE = Leo, VI = Virgo, LI = Libra, SC = Scorpio, SA = Sagittarius, CP = Capricorn, AQ = Aquarius, PI = Pisces

MOON SIGNS

Moon in Aries

You have a strong imagination, courage, determination and a desire to do things in your own way and forge your own path through life.

Originality is a key attribute; you are seldom stuck for ideas although your mind is changeable and you could take the time to focus on individual tasks. Often quick-tempered, you take orders from few people and live life at a fast pace. Avoid health problems by taking regular time out for rest and relaxation.

Emotionally, it is important that you talk to those you are closest to and work out your true feelings. Once you discover that people are there to help, there is less necessity for you to do everything yourself.

Moon in Taurus

The Moon in Taurus gives you a courteous and friendly manner, which means you are likely to have many friends.

The good things in life mean a lot to you, as Taurus is an Earth sign that delights in experiences which please the senses. Hence you are probably a lover of good food and drink, which may in turn mean you need to keep an eye on the bathroom scales, especially as looking good is also important to you.

Emotionally you are fairly stable and you stick by your own standards. Taureans do not respond well to change. Intuition also plays an important part in your life.

Moon in Gemini

You have a warm-hearted character, sympathetic and eager to help others. At times reserved, you can also be articulate and chatty: this is part of the paradox of Gemini, which always brings duplicity to the nature. You are interested in current affairs, have a good intellect, and are good company and likely to have many friends. Most of your friends have a high opinion of you and would be ready to defend you should the need arise. However, this is usually unnecessary, as you are quite capable of defending yourself in any verbal confrontation.

Travel is important to your inquisitive mind and you find intellectual stimulus in mixing with people from different cultures. You also gain much from reading, writing and the arts but you do need plenty of rest and relaxation in order to avoid fatigue.

Moon in Cancer

The Moon in Cancer at the time of birth is a fortunate position as Cancer is the Moon's natural home. This means that the qualities of compassion and understanding given by the Moon are especially enhanced in your nature, and you are friendly and sociable and cope well with emotional pressures. You cherish home and family life, and happily do the domestic tasks. Your surroundings are important to you and you hate squalor and filth. You are likely to have a love of music and poetry.

Your basic character, although at times changeable like the Moon itself, depends on symmetry. You aim to make your surroundings comfortable and harmonious, for yourself and those close to you.

Moon in Leo

The best qualities of the Moon and Leo come together to make you warmhearted, fair, ambitious and self-confident. With good organisational abilities, you invariably rise to a position of responsibility in your chosen career. This is fortunate as you don't enjoy being an 'also-ran' and would rather be an important part of a small organisation than a menial in a large one.

You should be lucky in love, and happy, provided you put in the effort to make a comfortable home for yourself and those close to you. It is likely that you will have a love of pleasure, sport, music and literature. Life brings you many rewards, most of them as a direct result of your own efforts, although you may be luckier than average and ready to make the best of any situation.

Moon in Virgo

You are endowed with good mental abilities and a keen receptive memory, but you are never ostentatious or pretentious. Naturally quite reserved, you still have many friends, especially of the opposite sex. Marital relationships must be discussed carefully and worked at so that they remain harmonious, as personal attachments can be a problem if you do not give them your full attention.

Talented and persevering, you possess artistic qualities and are a good homemaker. Earning your honours through genuine merit, you work long and hard towards your objectives but show little pride in your achievements. Many short journeys will be undertaken in your life.

Moon in Libra

With the Moon in Libra you are naturally popular and make friends easily. People like you, probably more than you realise, you bring fun to a party and are a natural diplomat. For all its good points, Libra is not the most stable of astrological signs and, as a result, your emotions can be a little unstable too. Therefore, although the Moon in Libra is said to be good for love and marriage, your Sun sign and Rising sign will have an important effect on your emotional and loving qualities.

You must remember to relate to others in your decision-making. Co-operation is crucial because Libra represents the 'balance' of life that can only be achieved through harmonious relationships. Conformity is not easy for you because Libra, an Air sign, likes its independence.

Moon in Scorpio

Some people might call you pushy. In fact, all you really want to do is to live life to the full and protect yourself and your family from the pressures of life. Take care to avoid giving the impression of being sarcastic or impulsive and use your energies wisely and constructively.

You have great courage and you invariably achieve your goals by force of personality and sheer effort. You are fond of mystery and are good at predicting the outcome of situations and events. Travel experiences can be beneficial to you.

You may experience problems if you do not take time to examine your motives in a relationship, and also if you allow jealousy, always a feature of Scorpio, to cloud your judgement.

Moon in Sagittarius

The Moon in Sagittarius helps to make you a generous individual with humanitarian qualities and a kind heart. Restlessness may be intrinsic as your mind is seldom still. Perhaps because of this, you have a need for change that could lead you to several major moves during your adult life. You are not afraid to stand your ground when you know your judgement is right, you speak directly and have good intuition.

At work you are quick, efficient and versatile and so you make an ideal employee. You need work to be intellectually demanding and do not enjoy tedious routines.

In relationships, you anger quickly if faced with stupidity or deception, though you are just as quick to forgive and forget. Emotionally, there are times when your heart rules your head.

Moon in Capricorn

The Moon in Capricorn makes you popular and likely to come into the public eye in some way. The watery Moon is not entirely comfortable in the Earth sign of Capricorn and this may lead to some difficulties in the early years of life. An initial lack of creative ability and indecision must be overcome before the true qualities of patience and perseverance inherent in Capricorn can show through.

You have good administrative ability and are a capable worker, and if you are careful you can accumulate wealth. But you must be cautious and take professional advice in partnerships, as you are open to deception. You may be interested in social or welfare work, which suit your organisational skills and sympathy for others.

Moon in Aquarius

The Moon in Aquarius makes you an active and agreeable person with a friendly, easy-going nature. Sympathetic to the needs of others, you flourish in a laid-back atmosphere. You are broad-minded, fair and open to suggestion, although sometimes you have an unconventional quality which others can find hard to understand.

You are interested in the strange and curious, and in old articles and places. You enjoy trips to these places and gain much from them. Political, scientific and educational work interests you and you might choose a career in science or technology.

Money-wise, you make gains through innovation and concentration and Lunar Aquarians often tackle more than one job at a time. In love you are kind and honest.

Moon in Pisces

You have a kind, sympathetic nature, somewhat retiring at times, but you always take account of others' feelings and help when you can.

Personal relationships may be problematic, but as life goes on you can learn from your experiences and develop a better understanding of yourself and the world around you.

You have a fondness for travel, appreciate beauty and harmony and hate disorder and strife. You may be fond of literature and would make a good writer or speaker yourself. You have a creative imagination and may come across as an incurable romantic. You have strong intuition, maybe bordering on a mediumistic quality, which sets you apart from the mass. You may not be rich in cash terms, but your personal gifts are worth more than gold.

CAPRICORN IN LOVE

Discover how compatible in love you are with people from the same and other signs of the zodiac. Five stars equals a match made in heaven!

Capricorn meets Capricorn

One of the best combinations because Capricorn knows what it wants and likes its partner to be the same. This may not be the deepest or most passionate of relationships, but Capricorn is adaptable enough to accept that. Material success is likely for this couple as they share the ability to move slowly towards even distant horizons. There will be words of love and a generally happy family atmosphere, and although at times the relationship may look lukewarm, it will usually remain strong and secure. Star rating: *****

Capricorn meets Aquarius

Probably one of the least likely combinations as Capricorn and Aquarius are unlikely to choose each other in the first place, unless one side is quite untypical of their sign. Capricorn approaches things in a practical way and likes to get things done, while Aquarius works almost exclusively for the moment and relies heavily on intuition. Their attitudes to romance are also diametrically opposed: Aquarius' moods tend to swing from red hot to ice cold in a minute, which is alien to steady Capricorn. Star rating: **

Capricorn meets Pisces

There is some chance of a happy relationship here, but it will need work on both sides. Capricorn is a go-getter, but likes to plan long term. Pisces is naturally more immediate, but has enough intuition to understand the Goat's thinking. Both have patience, but it will usually be Pisces who chooses to play second fiddle. The quiet nature of both signs might be a problem, as someone will have to lead, especially in social situations. Both signs should recognise this fact and accommodate it. Star rating: ***

Capricorn meets Aries

Capricorn works conscientiously to achieve its objectives and so can be the perfect companion for Aries. The Ram knows how to achieve but not how to consolidate, so the two signs have a great deal to offer one another practically. There may not be fireworks and it's sometimes doubtful how well they know each other, but it may not matter. Aries is outwardly hot but inwardly cool, whilst Capricorn can appear low-key but be a furnace underneath. Such a pairing can gradually find contentment, though both parties may wonder how this is so. Star rating: ****

Capricorn meets Taurus

If not quite a match made in heaven, this comes close. Both signs are Earthy in nature and that is a promising start. Capricorn is very practical and can make a Taurean's dreams come true. Both are tidy, like to know what is going to happen in a day-to-day sense, and are steady and committed. Taurus loves refinement, which Capricorn accepts and even helps to create. A good prognosis for material success rounds off a relationship that could easily stay the course. The only thing missing is a genuine sense of humour. Star rating: *****

Capricorn meets Gemini

Gemini has a natural fondness for Capricorn, which at first may be mutual. However, Capricorn is very organised, practical and persevering, and always achieves its goals in the end. Gemini starts out like this, but then starts to use a more instinctive and evolutionary approach, which may interfere with mutual objectives. To compensate, Gemini helps Capricorn avoid taking itself too seriously, while Capricorn brings a degree of stability into Gemini's world. When this pairing does work, though, it will be spectacular! Star rating: ***

Capricorn meets Cancer

Just about the only thing this pair have in common is the fact that both signs begin 'Ca'! Some signs of the zodiac are instigators and some are reactors, and both the Crab and the Goat are reactors. Consequently, they both need incentives from their partners but won't find it in each other and, with neither side taking the initiative, there's a spark missing. Cancer and Capricorn do think alike in some ways and so, if they can find their common purpose, they can be as happy as anyone. It's just rather unlikely. Star rating: **

Capricorn meets Leo

Despite promising appearances, this match often fails to take. Capricorn focuses on long-term objectives and, like Leo, is very practical. Both signs are capable of attaining success after a struggle, which, while requiring effort, gives them a mutual goal. But when life is easier, the cracks begin to show. Capricorn can be too serious for Leo, and the couple share few ideals. Leo loves luxury, Capricorn seeks austerity. Leo is warm but Capricorn seems cold and wintry in comparison. Both have many good points, but they don't seem to fire each other off properly. Star rating: **

Capricorn meets Virgo

One of the best possible combinations, because Virgo and Capricorn have an instinctive understanding. Both signs know the value of dedicated hard work and apply it equally in a relationship and other areas of life. Two of the most practical signs, nothing is beyond their ken, even if to outsiders they appear rather sterile or lacking in 'oomph'. What matters most is that the individuals are happy and with so much in common, the likelihood of mutual material success, and a shared devotion to home and family, there isn't much doubt of that. Star rating: *****

Capricorn meets Libra

Libra and Capricorn rub each other up the wrong way because their attitudes to life are so different, and although both are capable of doing something about this, in reality they probably won't. Capricorn is steady, determined and solid, while Libra is bright but sometimes superficial and not entirely reliable. They usually lack the instant spark needed to get them together in the first place, so when it does happen it is often because one of the partners is not very typical of their sign. Star rating: **

Capricorn meets Scorpio

Lack of communication is the governing factor here. Neither of this pair are renowned communicators and both need a partner to draw out their full verbal potential. Consequently, Scorpio may find Capricorn cold and unapproachable while Capricorn could find Scorpio dark and brooding. Both are naturally tidy and would keep a pristine house but great effort and a mutual goal is needed on both sides to overcome the missing spark. A good match on the financial side, but probably not an earthshattering personal encounter. Star rating: **

Capricorn meets Sagittarius

Any real problem here will stem from a lack of understanding. Capricorn is very practical and needs to be constantly on the go – though in a fairly low-key sort of way. Sagittarius is busy too, though always in a panic and invariably behind its deadlines, which will annoy organised Capricorn. Sagittarius doesn't really have the depth of nature that best suits an Earth sign like Capricorn and its flirty nature could upset the sensitive Goat, but their lighter attitude could be cheering, too. Star rating: ***

VENUS: THE PLANET OF LOVE

If you look up at the sky around sunset or sunrise you will often see Venus in close attendance to the Sun. It is arguably one of the most beautiful sights of all and there is little wonder that historically it became associated with the goddess of love. But although Venus is important in your attitude to love and in the way others see you romantically, this is only one of its spheres of influence.

Venus plays a part in the cultured side of your life and has much to do with your appreciation of art, literature, music and general creativity. Even the way you look is responsive to the part of the zodiac that Venus occupied at the start of your life, though this is also down to your Sun sign and Ascending sign. If, at the time you were born, Venus occupied one of the more gregarious zodiac signs, you will be open in love, as well as more attracted to entertainment, social gatherings and good company. If on the other hand Venus occupied a quiet zodiac sign at the time of your birth, you would tend to be more retiring and less willing to shine in public situations.

Venus can have a great bearing on your outward appearance and since we all have to mix with others, knowledge of Venus' position at your birth can help you learn to make the best of what it has to offer you.

One of the great complications in the past has always been trying to establish exactly what zodiac position Venus enjoyed when you were born because the planet is notoriously difficult to track. Here I have created an exclusive table for your Sun sign, shown opposite.

To calculate your Venus sign, first look up the year of your birth in the table. As Capricorn naturally spans two calendar years every time it comes around, double-check that you are looking at the right line. The table is organised so that December is always the first month, so, for instance, if you were born in December 1940 or January 1941 you would look at the column for 1940–1, because the year on the calendar has changed while the zodiac is still in the sign of Capricorn. If you were born in January 1942 you would look at the column for 1941–2. Once you have the right column, you will see a sign of the zodiac next to the date. This was the sign that Venus occupied in that year. If Venus occupied more than one sign during the period, this is indicated by the date on which the sign changed and the name of the new sign. For instance, if you are looking at the years 1940–1, Venus was in Sagittarius until the 15th January, after which time it was in Capricorn. If you were born before 15th January your Venus sign is Sagittarius, if you were born on or after 15th January, your Venus sign is Capricorn. Once you have established the position of Venus at the time of your birth, you can then look in the pages which follow to see how this has a bearing on your life.

1914–15 SCORPIO / 2.1 SAGITTARIUS
1915–16 CAPRICORN / 27.12 AQUARIUS / 20.1 PISCES
1916–17 SAGITTARIUS / 16.1 CAPRICORN
1917–18 AQUARIUS
1918–19 CAPRICORN / 10.1 AQUARIUS
1919–20 SCORPIO / 5.1 SAGITTARIUS
1920–1 AQUARIUS / 7.1 PISCES
1921–2 SAGITTARIUS / 30.12 CAPRICORN
1922–3 SCORPIO / 6.1 SAGITTARIUS
1923–4 CAPRICORN / 26.12 AQUARIUS / 19.1 PISCES
1924–5 SAGITTARIUS / 15.1 CAPRICORN
1925–6 AQUARIUS
1926–7 CAPRICORN / 9.1 AQUARIUS
1927–8 SCORPIO / 4.1 SAGITTARIUS
1928–9 AQUARIUS / 6.1 PISCES
1929–30 SAGITTARIUS / 29.12 CAPRICORN
1930–1 SCORPIO / 3.1 SAGITTARIUS
1931–2 CAPRICORN / 26.12 AQUARIUS / 19.1 PISCES
1932–3 SAGITTARIUS / 15.1 PISCES
1933–4 AQUARIUS
1934–5 CAPRICORN / 9.1 AQUARIUS
1935–6 SCORPIO / 4.1 SAGITTARIUS
1936–7 AQUARIUS / 6.1 PISCES
1937–8 SAGITTARIUS / 29.12 CAPRICORN
1938–9 SCORPIO / 3.1 SAGITTARIUS
1939–40 CAPRICORN / 25.12 AQUARIUS / 18.1 PISCES
1940–1 SAGITTARIUS / 15.1 CAPRICORN
1941–2 AQUARIUS
1942–3 CAPRICORN / 8.1 AQUARIUS
1943–4 SCORPIO / 3.1 SAGITTARIUS
1944–5 AQUARIUS / 5.1 PISCES
1945–6 SAGITTARIUS / 28.12 CAPRICORN
1946–7 SCORPIO / 3.1 SAGITTARIUS
1947–8 CAPRICORN / 25.12 AQUARIUS / 18.1 PISCES
1948–9 SAGITTARIUS /14.1 CAPRICORN
1949–50 AQUARIUS
1950–1 CAPRICORN / 8.1 AQUARIUS
1951–2 SCORPIO / 3.1 SAGITTARIUS
1952–3 AQUARIUS / 5.1 PISCES
1953–4 SAGITTARIUS / 28.12 CAPRICORN
1954–5 SCORPIO / 4.1 SAGITTARIUS
1955–6 CAPRICORN / 24.12 AQUARIUS / 17.1 PISCES
1956–7 SAGITTARIUS / 14.1 CAPRICORN
1957–8 AQUARIUS
1958–9 CAPRICORN / 7.1 AQUARIUS
1959–60 SCORPIO / 2.1 SAGITTARIUS
1960–1 AQUARIUS / 5.1 PISCES
1961–2 SAGITTARIUS / 1962–3 SCORPIO / 4.1 SAGITTARIUS
1963–4 CAPRICORN / 24.12 AQUARIUS / 17.1 PISCES
1964–5 SAGITTARIUS / 13.1 CAPRICORN
1965–6 AQUARIUS
1966–7 CAPRICORN / 7.1 AQUARIUS
1967–8 SCORPIO / 2.1 SAGITTARIUS
1968–9 AQUARIUS / 5.1 PISCES
1969–70 SAGITTARIUS / 27.12 CAPRICORN
1970–1 SCORPIO / 5.1 SAGITTARIUS
1971–2 CAPRICORN / 23.12 AQUARIUS / 16.1 PISCES
1972–3 SAGITTARIUS / 12.1 CAPRICORN
1973–4 AQUARIUS
1974–5 CAPRICORN / 6.1 AQUARIUS
1975–6 SCORPIO / 1.1 SAGITTARIUS
1976–7 AQUARIUS / 4.1 PISCES
1977–8 SAGITTARIUS / 27.12 CAPRICORN
1978–9 SCORPIO / 5.1 SAGITTARIUS
1979–80 CAPRICORN / 23.12 AQUARIUS / 16.1 PISCES
1980–1 SAGITTARIUS / 12.1 CAPRICORN
1981–2 AQUARIUS
1982–3 CAPRICORN / 6.1 AQUARIUS
1983–4 SCORPIO / 1.1 SAGITTARIUS
1984–5 AQUARIUS / 4.1 PISCES
1985–6 SAGITTARIUS / 27.12 CAPRICORN
1986–7 SCORPIO / 6.1 SAGITTARIUS
1987–8 AQUARIUS / 15.1 PISCES
1988–9 SAGITTARIUS / 11.1 CAPRICORN
1989–90 AQUARIUS / 17.1 CAPRICORN
1990–1 CAPRICORN / 5.1 AQUARIUS
1991–2 SCORPIO / 1.1 SAGITTARIUS
1992–3 AQUARIUS / 4.1 PISCES
1993–4 SAGITTARIUS / 26.12 CAPRICORN
1994–5 SCORPIO / 7.1 SAGITTARIUS
1995–6 AQUARIUS / 15.1 PISCES
1996–7. SAGITTARIUS / 11.1 CAPRICORN
1997–8 AQUARIUS / 14.1 CAPRICORN
1998–9 CAPRICORN / 5.1 AQUARIUS
1999–00 SCORPIO / 1.1 SAGITTARIUS
2000–01 SAGITTARIUS / 26.12 CAPRICORN
2001–02 CAPRICORN / 4.1 AQUARIUS
2002–03 SAGITTARIUS / 26.12 CAPRICORN
2003–04 SCORPIO / 7.1 SAGITTARIUS
2004–05 SAGITTARIUS / 30.12 CAPRICORN
2006–07 AQUARIUS / 14.1 CAPRICORN
2007–08 CAPRICORN / 5.1 AQUARIUS
2008–09 SCORPIO / 1.1 SAGITTARIUS
2009–10 SAGITTARIUS / 26.12 CAPRICORN
2010–11 SAGITTARIUS / 26.12 CAPRICORN
2011–12 CAPRICORN / 4.12 AQUARIUS
2012–13 AQUARIUS / 14.1 CAPRICORN

VENUS THROUGH THE ZODIAC SIGNS

Venus in Aries

Amongst other things, the position of Venus in Aries indicates a fondness for travel, music and all creative pursuits. Your nature tends to be affectionate and you would try not to create confusion or difficulty for others if it could be avoided. Many people with this planetary position have a great love of the theatre, and mental stimulation is of the greatest importance. Early romantic attachments are common with Venus in Aries, so it is very important to establish a genuine sense of romantic continuity. Early marriage is not recommended, especially if it is based on sympathy. You may give your heart a little too readily on occasions.

Venus in Taurus

You are capable of very deep feelings and your emotions tend to last for a very long time. This makes you a trusting partner and lover, whose constancy is second to none. In life you are precise and careful and always try to do things the right way. Although this means an ordered life, which you are comfortable with, it can also lead you to be rather too fussy for your own good. Despite your pleasant nature, you are very fixed in your opinions and quite able to speak your mind. Others are attracted to you and historical astrologers always quoted this position of Venus as being very fortunate in terms of marriage. However, if you find yourself involved in a failed relationship, it could take you a long time to trust again.

Venus in Gemini

As with all associations related to Gemini, you tend to be quite versatile, anxious for change and intelligent in your dealings with the world at large. You may gain money from more than one source but you are equally good at spending it. There is an inference here that you are a good communicator, via either the written or the spoken word, and you love to be in the company of interesting people. Always on the look-out for culture, you may also be very fond of music, and love to indulge the curious and cultured side of your nature. In romance you tend to have more than one relationship and could find yourself associated with someone who has previously been a friend or even a distant relative.

Venus in Cancer

You often stay close to home because you are very fond of family and enjoy many of your most treasured moments when you are with those you love. Being naturally sympathetic, you will always do anything you can to support those around you, even people you hardly know at all. This charitable side of your nature is your most noticeable trait and is one of the reasons why others are naturally so fond of you. Being receptive and in some cases even psychic, you can see through to the soul of most of those with whom you come into contact. You may not commence too many romantic attachments but when you do give your heart, it tends to be unconditionally.

Venus in Leo

It must become quickly obvious to almost anyone you meet that you are kind, sympathetic and yet determined enough to stand up for anyone or anything that is truly important to you. Bright and sunny, you warm the world with your natural enthusiasm and would rarely do anything to hurt those around you, or at least not intentionally. In romance you are ardent and sincere, though some may find your style just a little overpowering. Gains come through your contacts with other people and this could be especially true with regard to romance, for love and money often come hand in hand for those who were born with Venus in Leo. People claim to understand you, though you are more complex than you seem.

Venus in Virgo

Your nature could well be fairly quiet no matter what your Sun sign might be, though this fact often manifests itself as an inner peace and would not prevent you from being basically sociable. Some delays and even the odd disappointment in love cannot be ruled out with this planetary position, though it's a fact that you will usually find the happiness you look for in the end. Catapulting yourself into romantic entanglements that you know to be rather ill-advised is not sensible, and it would be better to wait before you committed yourself exclusively to any one person. It is the essence of your nature to serve the world at large and through doing so it is possible that you will attract money at some stage in your life.

Venus in Libra

Venus is very comfortable in Libra and bestows upon those people who have this planetary position a particular sort of kindness that is easy to recognise. This is a very good position for all sorts of friendships and also for romantic attachments that usually bring much joy into your life. Few individuals with Venus in Libra would avoid marriage and since you are capable of great depths of love, it is likely that you will find a contented personal life. You like to mix with people of integrity and intelligence but don't take kindly to scruffy surroundings or work that means getting your hands too dirty. Careful speculation, good business dealings and money through marriage all seem fairly likely.

Venus in Scorpio

You are quite open and tend to spend money quite freely, even on those occasions when you don't have very much. Although your intentions are always good, there are times when you get yourself in to the odd scrape and this can be particularly true when it comes to romance, which you may come to late or from a rather unexpected direction. Certainly you have the power to be happy and to make others contented on the way, but you find the odd stumbling block on your journey through life and it could seem that you have to work harder than those around you. As a result of this, you gain a much deeper understanding of the true value of personal happiness than many people ever do, and are likely to achieve true contentment in the end.

Venus in Sagittarius

You are lighthearted, cheerful and always able to see the funny side of any situation. These facts enhance your popularity, which is especially high with members of the opposite sex. You should never have to look too far to find romantic interest in your life, though it is just possible that you might be too willing to commit yourself before you are certain that the person in question is right for you. Part of the problem here extends to other areas of life too. The fact is that you like variety in everything and so can tire of situations that fail to offer it. All the same, if you choose wisely and learn to understand your restless side, then great happiness can be yours.

Venus in Capricorn

The most notable trait that comes from Venus in this position is that it makes you trustworthy and able to take on all sorts of responsibilities in life. People are instinctively fond of you and love you all the more because you are always ready to help those who are in any form of need. Social and business popularity can be yours and there is a magnetic quality to your nature that is particularly attractive in a romantic sense. Anyone who wants a partner for a lover, a spouse and a good friend too would almost certainly look in your direction. Constancy is the hallmark of your nature and unfaithfulness would go right against the grain. You might sometimes be a little too trusting.

Venus in Aquarius

This location of Venus offers a fondness for travel and a desire to try out something new at every possible opportunity. You are extremely easy to get along with and tend to have many friends from varied backgrounds, classes and inclinations. You like to live a distinct sort of life and gain a great deal from moving about, both in a career sense and with regard to your home. It is not out of the question that you could form a romantic attachment to someone who comes from far away or be attracted to a person of a distinctly artistic and original nature. What you cannot stand is jealousy, for you have friends of both sexes and would want to keep things that way.

Venus in Pisces

The first thing people tend to notice about you is your wonderful, warm smile. Being very charitable by nature you will do anything to help others, even if you don't know them well. Much of your life may be spent sorting out situations for other people, but it is very important to feel that you are living for yourself too. In the main, you remain cheerful, and tend to be quite attractive to members of the opposite sex. Where romantic attachments are concerned, you could be drawn to people who are significantly older or younger than yourself or to someone with a unique career or point of view. It might be best for you to avoid marrying whilst you are still very young.

THE ASTRAL DIARY

HOW THE DIAGRAMS WORK

Through the picture diagrams in the Astral Diary I want to help you to plot your year. With them you can see where the positive and negative aspects will be found in each month. To make the most of them, all you have to do is remember where and when!

Let me show you how they work ...

THE MONTH AT A GLANCE

Just as there are twelve separate zodiac signs, so astrologers believe that each sign has twelve separate aspects to life. Each of the twelve segments relates to a different personal aspect. I list them all every month so that their meanings are always clear.

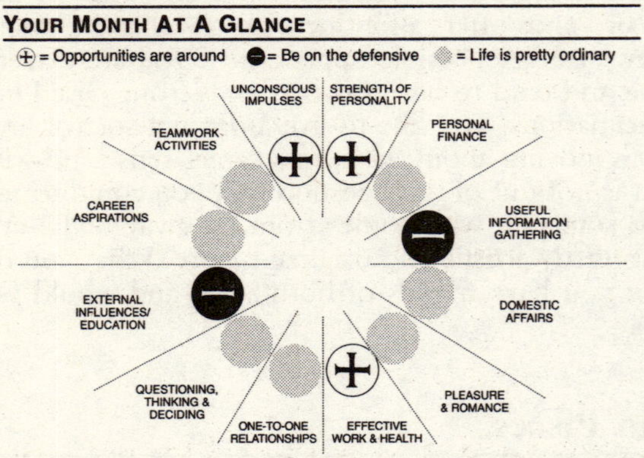

I have designed this chart to show you how and when these twelve different aspects are being influenced throughout the year. When there is a shaded circle, nothing out of the ordinary is to be expected. However, when a circle turns white with a plus sign, the influence is positive. Where the circle is black with a minus sign, it is a negative.

YOUR ENERGY RHYTHM CHART

On the opposite page is a picture diagram in which I link your zodiac group to the rhythm of the Moon. In doing this I have calculated when you will be gaining strength from its influence and equally when you may be weakened by it.

If you think of yourself as being like the tides of the ocean then you may understand how your own energies must also rise and fall. And if you understand how it works and when it is working, then you can better organise your activities to achieve more and get things done more easily.

YOUR ENERGY RHYTHM CHART

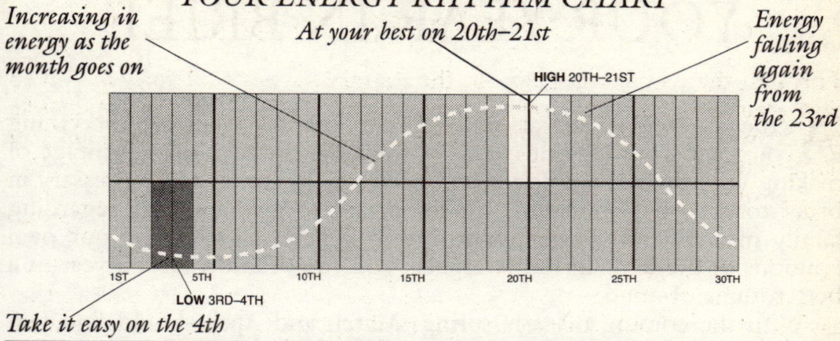

MOVING PICTURE SCREEN

Love, money, career and vitality measured every week

The diagram at the end of each week is designed to be informative and fun. The arrows move up and down the scale to give you an idea of the strength of your opportunities in each area. If LOVE stands at plus 4, then get out and put yourself about because things are going your way in romance! The further down the arrow goes, the weaker the opportunities. Do note that the diagram is an overall view of your astrological aspects and therefore reflects a trend which may not concur with every day in that cycle.

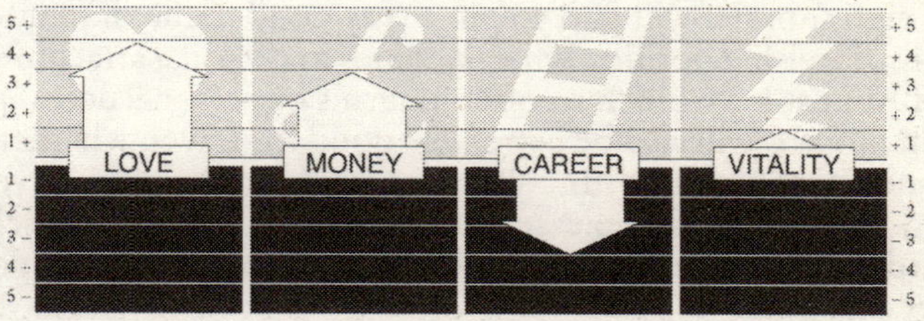

AND FINALLY:

am ....

pm ....

The two lines that are left blank in each daily entry of the Astral Diary are for your own personal use. You may find them ideal for keeping a check on birthdays or appointments, though it could also be an idea to make notes from the astrological trends and diagrams a few weeks in advance. Some of the lines are marked with a key, which indicates the working of astrological cycles in your life. Look out for them each week as they are the best days to take action or make decisions. The daily text tells you which area of your life to focus on.

☿ = Mercury is retrograde on that day.

CAPRICORN: YOUR YEAR IN BRIEF

As the year begins, January and February may not offer you everything you want from life but trends at this time do have the advantage of making you extremely efficient and willing to go as far as is necessary in order to get what you want. It's important to give and take regarding family matters and also at work, but you need to stick to your own opinions in the end. In most respects you could hardly start a year in a better frame of mind.

With the coming of early spring, March and April should find you anxious to get on with things, even when those around you are more reticent. There are financial gains to be made, especially during March, with April seeing you in a position to consolidate these gains. Routines won't appeal to you too much at this time but you will remain at your practical best in most things.

May and June continue the generally favourable trends, even if there are a few delays and small disappointments to deal with too. None of these should hold you up for long and you are so good at working through or round potential pitfalls that you may not even notice them. This is not the best time for financial risks or for pushing yourself too hard. In terms of your personal life you may be taking time out to look at relationships in a fresh and interesting way.

The high summer will find you in a very good frame of mind and in an especially promising position when it comes to personal attachments. Both July and August have much to offer in terms of personal accomplishment and both months will also be extremely good for travel, whether for work or pleasure. Get onside with colleagues, and be prepared in your home life to go the extra yard to please those you care about. Don't sell yourself short and trust yourself to rely on your intuition, which is particularly strong at this time.

September and October are likely to be months filled with enterprise and possibilities. Not everything you want is likely to be coming your way – or at least this might seem to be the case at first. In the main, you deal with all eventualities in your usual, efficient way and you have a distinct advantage at this time when it comes to working out what people around you are thinking.

The last two months of the year, November and December, have plenty to offer in terms of personal happiness and you will make a great deal more of Christmas this time around than would often be the case. November sees you anxious to make progress at work, whilst December reverberates with personal possibilities and should offer more in the way of romance. A happy and satisfying note on which to end a good year.

January 2012

Your Month at a Glance

⊕ = Opportunities are around ⊖ = Be on the defensive ● = Life is pretty ordinary

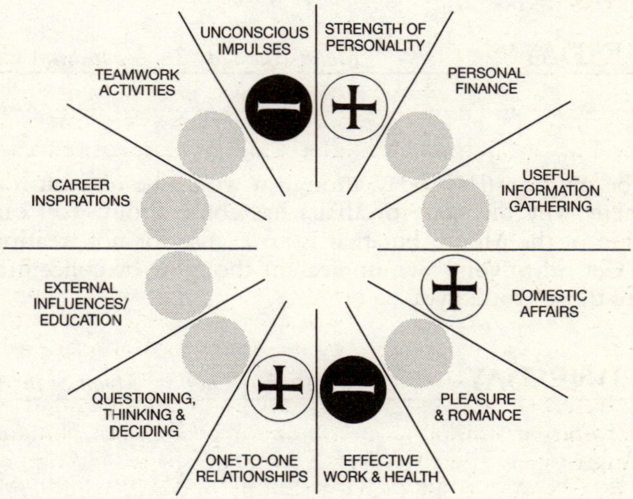

January Highs and Lows

Here I show you how the rhythms of the Moon will affect you this month. Like the tide, your energies and abilities will rise and fall with its pattern. When it is above the centre line, go for it, when it is below, you should be resting.

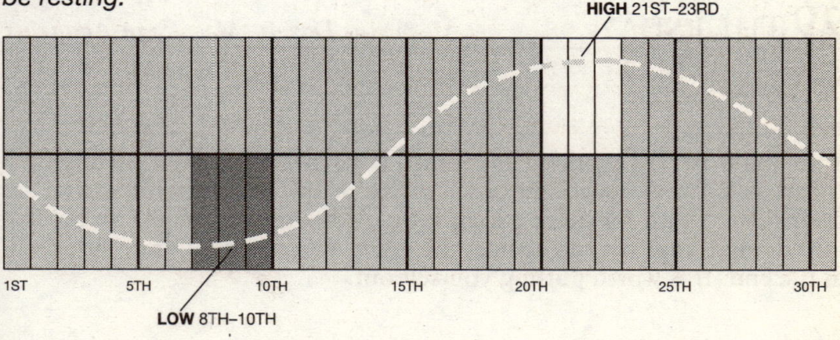

26 MONDAY *Moon Age Day 1 Moon Sign Capricorn*

am..

pm..

Things continue to be hectic but good fun. You won't have very much truck with rules and regulations today, even those set down by family members, and it might be said that you are something of an anarchist for the moment. Still, everyone will love your impish sense of humour and your determination to get everyone joining in.

27 TUESDAY *Moon Age Day 2 Moon Sign Capricorn*

am..

pm..

You can be quite restless today, though it would be difficult for you to know exactly why this state of affairs has come about. You can blame the position of the Moon, but that is no excuse for not treating others properly. Get rid of your own unpleasant thoughts by concentrating on the lives of those around you.

28 WEDNESDAY *Moon Age Day 3 Moon Sign Aquarius*

am..

pm..

You could be in quite a hurry to complete a particular project and will be very anxious not to allow anything to get in your way. In all probability this is something you should have done days or weeks ago, but today is hardly the right time to address it. Put it on the shelf until after the New Year and go on having fun.

29 THURSDAY *Moon Age Day 4 Moon Sign Aquarius*

am..

pm..

Your mind is now working overtime. Love affairs are well highlighted today, as is travel, maybe in order to see people you haven't shared an hour or two with for quite a long time. Although you might be bullied into doing things that go against the grain, you could be quite surprised in the end. It is worth putting yourself out.

30 FRIDAY *Moon Age Day 5 Moon Sign Pisces*

am ....

pm ....

The time is right to establish good relations with people around you, even those who have not been your favourites in the past. There is a good chance that you are being taken more seriously now and that you might attract, as a friend, someone who was never previously very kind to you. It's time to forgive and forget.

31 SATURDAY *Moon Age Day 6 Moon Sign Pisces*

am ....

pm ....

It seems as though enthusiasm remains at a peak and this is certainly no bad way to end a year. All you are really interested in today is having fun, together with making it possible for those around you to have a good time too. New Year resolutions may be put on hold because the enjoyment is hardly likely to stop at midnight.

1 SUNDAY *Moon Age Day 7 Moon Sign Aries*

am ....

pm ....

There is a deep and profound spirituality about your thinking at the moment, which is probably why others are seeking you out for help and advice. However long a particular task takes is the time you have to spend on it. That is self-evident to you, but probably not so in the case of other people.

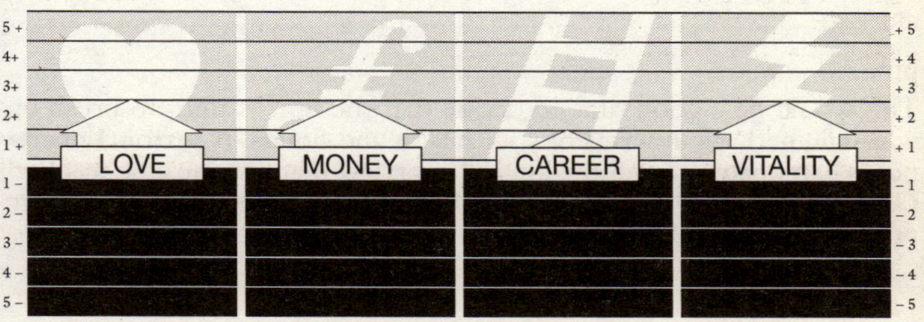

2 MONDAY *Moon Age Day 8 Moon Sign Aries*

am ....

pm ....

Enjoy yourself doing those things that suit you but don't get too carried away with routines and traditions. Times are changing and you have to alter with them. This is an excellent time for putting your point of view across to others. Once you have stated your case, allow matters to rest and don't push issues too much.

3 TUESDAY *Moon Age Day 9 Moon Sign Taurus*

am ....

pm ....

The Moon is now in your zodiac sign. That means a get-up-and-go sort of period so one during which you should put your high levels of energy to good use and enjoy the irrepressible desire to be out there in the mainstream of life. In terms of experiences, quality is as important as quality, though you should try to get a little of both today.

4 WEDNESDAY *Moon Age Day 10 Moon Sign Taurus*

am ....

pm ....

Most Capricorns will now be very difficult to hold back and tend to get the most out of any situation, especially social offers. Right now a good deal of your energy should be channelled into work-related matters. Whatever you do, you should remain determined to look and plan ahead.

5 THURSDAY *Moon Age Day 11 Moon Sign Taurus*

am ....

pm ....

This would be a good time to decide that the time is right to brush up your life, perhaps in terms of your health and fitness. A personal matter needs extra patience and the kind of overview that you are able to offer. Gear at least some of your thinking towards the home and allow more practical aspects to take a back seat.

6 FRIDAY *Moon Age Day 12 Moon Sign Gemini*

am ....

pm ....

Socially or professionally, it seems that you are in full flow and your powers of communication are emphasised as a result, so it would be good to seek out large gatherings. This isn't the time you would choose to take a day off, though be careful not to burn the candle at both ends more than is good for you.

7 SATURDAY *Moon Age Day 13 Moon Sign Gemini*

am ....

pm ....

It might be said that getting what you want from life today is more important than almost anything else. Unfortunately, this makes you sound quite selfish, which isn't the case at all. On the contrary, most of what you want involves a better life for others, even if you do feather your own nest on the way.

8 SUNDAY *Moon Age Day 14 Moon Sign Cancer*

am ....

pm ....

The simpler side of life is what seems to appeal to you most today, so – whatever the weather – try to spend at least some time in the fresh air, even if it is only a walk in the local park. A healthier sort of Capricorn now begins to emerge and more time spent outdoors could form part of your new year strategy.

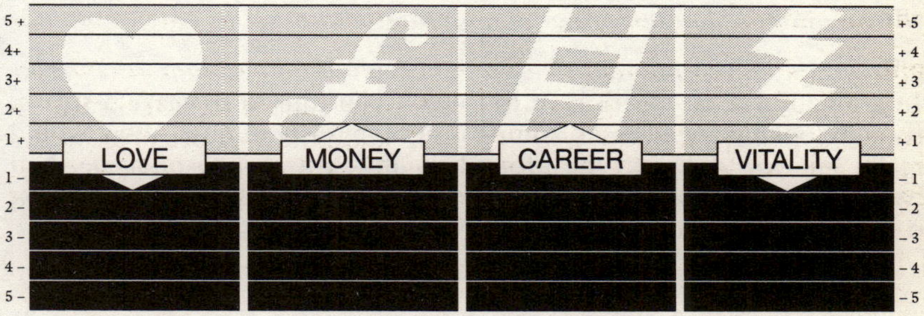

9 MONDAY *Moon Age Day 15 Moon Sign Cancer*

am ....

pm ....

The position of the Moon could put a slight damper on particular wishes you have for today. For example, there is no point in trying to undertake major projects. Things will come right in due course, but that's not likely to be today. Simply enjoy sitting and watching the river of life.

10 TUESDAY *Moon Age Day 16 Moon Sign Cancer*

am ....

pm ....

It would be a good time to concentrate on money matters at some stage today. Get out and about as much as you can, as you will benefit from mixing with others. In any case, a change is as good as a rest, particularly if that means you are coming together with the sort of people who find you very attractive.

11 WEDNESDAY *Moon Age Day 17 Moon Sign Leo*

am ....

pm ....

Try to make your home more comfortable and listen to family members who have an important story to tell. This is a forward-looking period and one that finds you much more in the mainstream of life. As you rush on towards specific objectives, it is clear that you know what you want from life and how to go about getting it.

12 THURSDAY *Moon Age Day 18 Moon Sign Leo*

am ....

pm ....

In a practical sense, there isn't too much you can do to make a splash, though looking ahead and planning is never a waste of time. What would really suit you down to the ground would be a change of scene. You would probably make the most of today if you focus your attention on romance and personal relationships.

13 FRIDAY *Moon Age Day 19 Moon Sign Virgo*

am ....

pm ....

There are people around who are in an excellent position to lend you a hand and you should not be too proud to make use of their services. Look out for a distinct advantage at work today, and don't be afraid to exploit it for all you are worth. When it comes to spending money, you need to be just a little careful.

14 SATURDAY *Moon Age Day 20 Moon Sign Virgo*

am ....

pm ....

Apply your ingenuity today – perhaps you can solve a problem by lateral thinking. Future plans can give you a shot in the arm as the weekend approaches. In fact, most of you will have finished the working week with a flourish and though not all the news appears to be good, you can get the best from it all.

15 SUNDAY *Moon Age Day 21 Moon Sign Libra*

am ....

pm ....

It is a fact that there are times to argue and there are periods when it is better to keep your counsel. The latter is the case right now, so don't get involved in trouble unless it is unavoidable. However, if you have no choice but to express your opinions, you should do so with all the clarity and conviction presently in your arsenal.

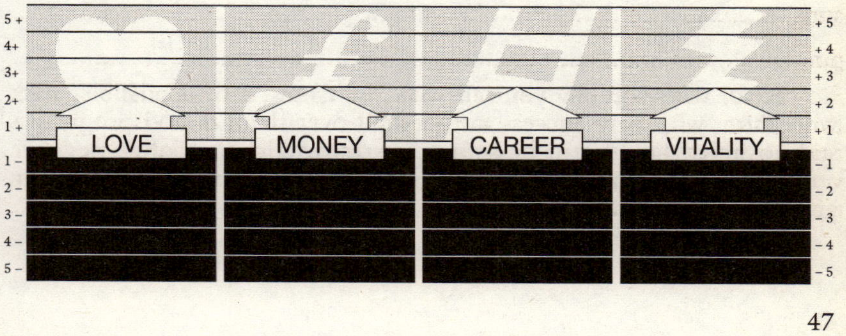

16 MONDAY *Moon Age Day 22 Moon Sign Libra*

am ....

pm..

You should make sure you display a very positive attitude, especially at work, as it might lead to you being singled out for some significant attention from superiors. Extra responsibilities are not out of the question. Although it might sometimes appear that the progress you make is limited, nothing could be further from the truth.

17 TUESDAY *Moon Age Day 23 Moon Sign Scorpio*

am ....

pm..

Convictions are important today, but don't take them to extremes. There are some exciting and interesting possibilities in store for you at present. Look around you and see where life wants to take you, because you can get much of what you want without having to try very hard.

18 WEDNESDAY *Moon Age Day 24 Moon Sign Scorpio*

am ....

pm..

Be willing to stand up for someone who is in trouble, even if you have to put yourself out significantly to do so. There are some strong supporting elements around now and you are able to make use of them. The fact is that one or two people think a great deal of you, and are willing to say so in public situations.

19 THURSDAY *Moon Age Day 25 Moon Sign Sagittarius*

am ....

pm..

Be careful who you ally yourself with right now and, if possible, stick with those who have success tattooed all over them. Good progress is still possible, though can be somewhat restricted by a slightly negative attitude on your part if you are mixing with people who seem reticent to give their all to situations.

20 FRIDAY *Moon Age Day 26 Moon Sign Sagittarius*

am ....

pm ....

Creative potential is good, especially around the home, but you also need to have hobbies and pastimes of your own, which is something to think about now. Confidence is lacking in projects you don't understand, which is why it would be sensible for the moment to stick to some good old favourites.

21 SATURDAY *Moon Age Day 27 Moon Sign Capricorn*

am ....

pm ....

The lunar high brings you to a situation that simply demands total involvement. There are ways to save money today, yet at the same time to enjoy yourself. Offer the sort of commitment to friends that you know they deserve, and be prepared for the rush of popularity that comes your way as a result.

22 SUNDAY *Moon Age Day 28 Moon Sign Capricorn*

am ....

pm ....

You have power on your side now. You may refuse to compromise on those occasions when you are certain that you are right. There are possible gains financially, plus you have a good eye for a bargain. For these reasons, you might decide that today would be good for shopping. If you overspend just a little – well, you can make up for it later.

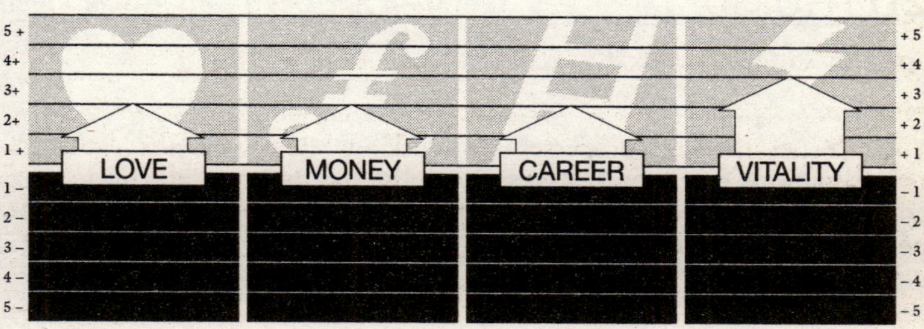

23 MONDAY *Moon Age Day 0 Moon Sign Capricorn*

am ....

pm ....

You could easily find today to be a day to count your blessings and to be glad for relationships that bring you warmth and satisfaction. Find the time to say one or two words that you don't normally have time to think about, and be prepared to help family members who are stuck out in the cold for some reason.

24 TUESDAY *Moon Age Day 1 Moon Sign Aquarius*

am ....

pm ....

Capricorns like to keep busy, and with creative potential good at the moment, it would be a good time to be decorating your home or helping with practical projects at a friend's house. What you really need today is to avoid being surprised by issues you don't understand. You tend to think deeply at this stage of the month.

25 WEDNESDAY *Moon Age Day 2 Moon Sign Aquarius*

am ....

pm ....

You won't become a millionaire today, but if you keep your wits about you there is a possibility you could take the first step. Small, unexpected gains are there for the taking. You are never anyone's fool but at the moment your perceptions are razor sharp. Use strong intuition when assessing others.

26 THURSDAY *Moon Age Day 3 Moon Sign Pisces*

am ....

pm ....

Your deeper thought processes are working really well now, so mull over situations carefully. If necessary, enlist the direct intervention of a colleague. There are times when maximum effort is necessary and other periods when you should take things slowly and steadily.

27 FRIDAY *Moon Age Day 4 Moon Sign Pisces*

am..

pm..

Don't leave your work alone until you are sure you have everything sorted to your satisfaction. The last day of the working week for many of you could be the most important. This is a pivotal time and a period during which you should be putting the finishing touches to some very important plans.

28 SATURDAY *Moon Age Day 5 Moon Sign Aries*

am..

pm..

It's a fact that many Capricorns will be finding ways and means to take a break of some sort at any time now. This is likely to be the case if you have been working especially hard. Enjoy whatever delights the weekend has to offer. Yours is a winter-born sign which means that the cold weather doesn't bother you very much.

29 SUNDAY *Moon Age Day 6 Moon Sign Aries*

am..

pm..

This might seem an uneventful sort of day but the planets suggest that it is the things that are happening below the surface you should be watching carefully. Close personal ties should be working well for you now. Stick to paths you understand for the moment but prepare yourself for a major push before long.

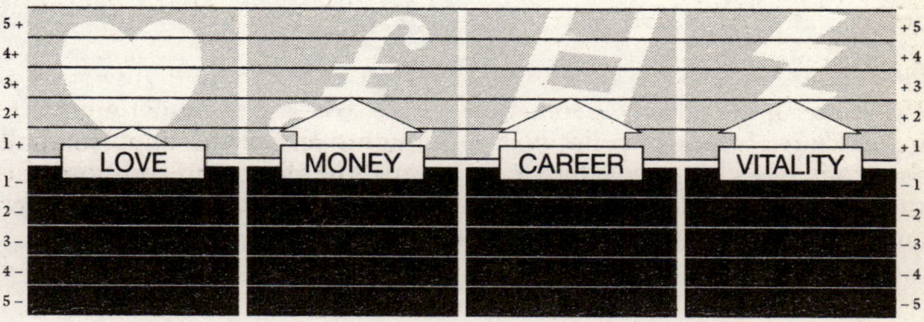

30 MONDAY *Moon Age Day 7 Moon Sign Aries*

am ....

pm ....

You have energy to spare so it would be sensible to keep busy – preferably on important projects – rather than putting off tasks until a later date. You are likely to be feeling quite determined, but try not to dig your heels in too far if colleagues can demonstrate that theirs is the right point of view.

31 TUESDAY *Moon Age Day 8 Moon Sign Taurus*

am ....

pm ....

Though you are more than ready to form new contacts of one sort or another today, you should avoid 'coming on too strong' in specific situations. Confidence is important, but you might give certain people the wrong impression. A healthy dose of your natural humility will do more for you now than a brash approach.

1 WEDNESDAY *Moon Age Day 9 Moon Sign Taurus*

am ....

pm ....

It's the first day of a new month, and perhaps also the first time that you have stopped to consider that this is a new year, filled with enterprise. You ought to be quite optimistic right now and willing to take certain situations by the scruff of the neck. Maintain a sense of proportion regarding romantic happenings.

2 THURSDAY *Moon Age Day 10 Moon Sign Gemini*

am ....

pm ....

No matter how unlikely it sometimes looks, you can engender a greater influence over your own life now. Although many of the opportunities that come your way today prove to be small in scope, the end result of them is likely to prove very positive. It is all a matter of looking carefully and then concentrating on one task at a time.

3 FRIDAY *Moon Age Day 11 Moon Sign Gemini*

am...

pm...

You should find people are listening to what you have to say and responding in a very positive way, so make sure what you say is worth hearing. You can contribute to your own success in a host of ways with these communication skills and the fact that you can impress almost anyone you meet. Career developments are on an upward spiral.

4 SATURDAY *Moon Age Day 12 Moon Sign Gemini*

am...

pm...

If there is one area of life that doesn't look quite as happy and solid as others, it could be related to your love life. You need to have a heart-to-heart with your partner, or someone else who has a bearing on your emotions. You will be surprised at just how much better you feel once you have spoken your mind.

5 SUNDAY *Moon Age Day 13 Moon Sign Cancer*

am...

pm...

You cannot get away entirely from the presence of the lunar low today. For a sign such as Capricorn the presence of the Moon in your opposite zodiac sign is not always particularly apparent. However, you may notice that life is not proceeding quite as smoothly as has recently been the case and extra effort is required.

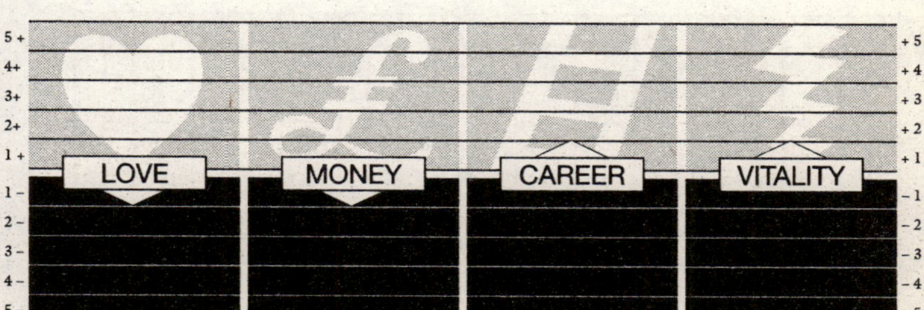

February 2012

Your Month at a Glance

⊕ = Opportunities are around ⊖ = Be on the defensive ● = Life is pretty ordinary

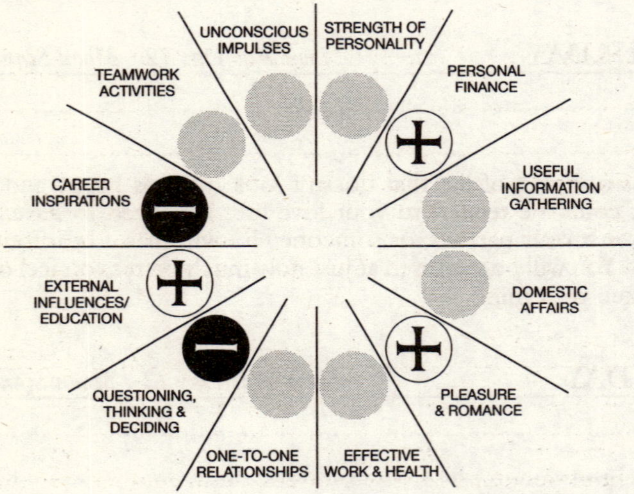

February Highs and Lows

Here I show you how the rhythms of the Moon will affect you this month. Like the tide, your energies and abilities will rise and fall with its pattern. When it is above the centre line, go for it, when it is below, you should be resting.

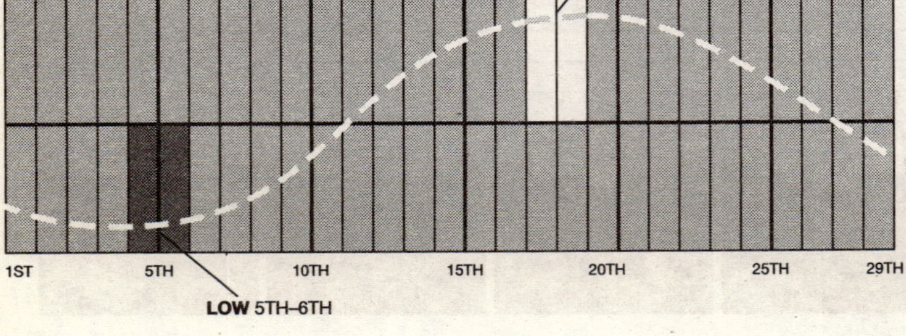

6 MONDAY *Moon Age Day 14 Moon Sign Cancer*

am ....

pm..

If you can summon up an extra dose of enthusiasm, it will get you through any minor difficulties now. Look out for new incentives coming your way before the day is out, which probably relate to the social aspects of your life. That should counter the feeling that not everything is working out entirely as you might wish.

7 TUESDAY *Moon Age Day 15 Moon Sign Leo*

am ....

pm..

You need to be innovative and to think on your feet. People you haven't seen for ages are likely to come back into your life at this time and might bring some important news with them. Self-confidence isn't lacking, but the means to get everything you want from life may not be present today.

8 WEDNESDAY *Moon Age Day 16 Moon Sign Leo*

am ....

pm..

An element of wanderlust is especially evident in your nature now – more than it has been for a while. However your travels might be more in your head than in reality, because the present position of the Moon is inclined to make you rather reticent about going far afield for the moment.

9 THURSDAY *Moon Age Day 17 Moon Sign Virgo*

am ....

pm..

If you are bored by conforming to expectations, try going out of your way to surprise people. Your personality profile is running high and this is definitely the right time to go for what you want. Few people would refuse you at present, and where awkward types do appear, your natural personality can bring them round in a flash.

10 FRIDAY *Moon Age Day 18 Moon Sign Virgo*

am ....

pm ....

Whilst you don't have absolute control over situations today, especially in a professional sense, you can make the best of what you are in terms of personality. This should ensure that you get on generally well by exercising your silver-tongued eloquence, which will surprise few, but charm everyone.

11 SATURDAY *Moon Age Day 19 Moon Sign Libra*

am ....

pm ....

Confidence remains intact for much of the weekend, though you might find one or two problems coming from the direction of family members. If this turns out to be the case, solve them as early in the day as you can. After that, you will feel the need for a change of scene and for social diversity.

12 SUNDAY *Moon Age Day 20 Moon Sign Libra*

am ....

pm ....

This may not be the most exciting day you will ever know, but it can be fairly solid all the same. Don't try anything too outrageous, and if you have to work, follow the lead of people who are in the know. Keep your ideas to yourself for today, but be prepared to put them into practice soon.

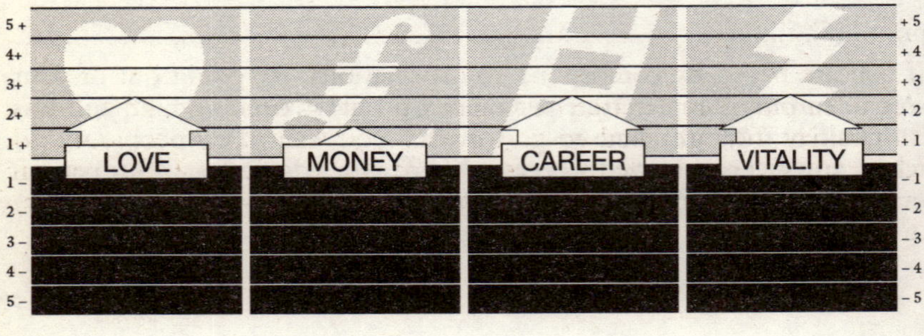

13 MONDAY *Moon Age Day 21 Moon Sign Scorpio*

am ....

pm ....

Make the most of the day by telling yourself you can find ways to have fun. A little cloud can stand over your head if you don't get the level of attention that you think is due to you at present. This is the less favourable side of Capricorn showing and you need to strive hard to avoid either selfishness or sulking.

14 TUESDAY *Moon Age Day 22 Moon Sign Scorpio*

am ....

pm ....

Make the most of what life offers and be certain that you show your partner how important they are to you. Changes to your home surroundings may seem interesting now. Tuesday brings changes of pace. In spheres of your life where things have been quiet, they now speed up, whereas in professional matters, there is a decline.

15 WEDNESDAY *Moon Age Day 23 Moon Sign Scorpio*

am ....

pm ....

Planning for the medium and longer-term future is something that Capricorn is extremely good at doing. You may be far more involved with minor tasks than you could possibly have imagined today, though it is important not to lose sight of the bigger picture.

16 THURSDAY *Moon Age Day 24 Moon Sign Sagittarius*

am ....

pm ....

A wilder and more carefree Capricorn subject is likely to meet the dawn of this day. You are filled with prospects for excitement and should not allow any given obstacle to get in your way for very long. Arguments are not helpful now, especially in the family. Do just about anything you can to avoid them.

17 FRIDAY *Moon Age Day 25 Moon Sign Sagittarius*

am ....

pm..

Getting exactly what you want from others or from life as a whole may not be very easy today and the result could be more than a little frustration. Don't aim this at others and do your best to realise that these are very temporary issues. By as early as tomorrow you will be able to turn situations around.

18 SATURDAY *Moon Age Day 26 Moon Sign Capricorn*

am ....

pm..

The Moon is in your zodiac sign, bringing the lunar high, that time during each month when you are emotionally and physically motivated. Undertake anything you decide to do today with a great deal of enthusiasm and plenty of determination. What is more, you have Lady Luck on your side.

19 SUNDAY *Moon Age Day 27 Moon Sign Capricorn*

am ....

pm..

It's time to get moving and there is very little at the moment that would be likely to hold you back. Keep a sense of proportion, but at the same time show a willingness to take the sort of risks that can get you ahead of the field. As the day moves onward, so the Moon has more and more of a part to play in your thinking and your successes.

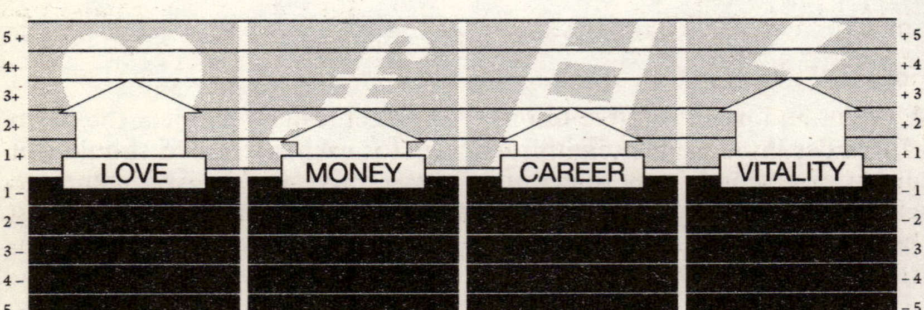

20 MONDAY *Moon Age Day 28 Moon Sign Aquarius*

am ....

pm ....

A great deal of helpful input is on the way and you merely have to listen to what family members and friends are saying in order to benefit. It would be advisable not to assume you have all the answers yourself. This would be a very good period for working in conjunction with others on practical projects.

21 TUESDAY *Moon Age Day 29 Moon Sign Aquarius*

am ....

pm ....

This is probably the best single day for professional and practical progress during the whole of February. The Moon is particularly helpful to your efforts at the moment, though much of what you need comes from others, one or two of whom appear to feel they are somehow in your debt and want to help you all they can.

22 WEDNESDAY *Moon Age Day 0 Moon Sign Pisces*

am ....

pm ....

It could seem that you have lessons to learn in the sphere of romance. Perhaps you haven't been quite as attentive as you should or it is possible that the practical necessities of life have prevented you from spending as much time with your lover as you would have wished. Now you can put things right.

23 THURSDAY *Moon Age Day 1 Moon Sign Pisces*

am ....

pm ....

The most important intention for you at present is to have fun, which might not be very easy during the working week. However, with extra effort you can turn the most mundane situations into ones that please both yourself and those around you. Ego energies rise to the surface more than ever at the moment.

24 FRIDAY *Moon Age Day 2 Moon Sign Pisces*

am ....

pm ....

A little trip to see friends might be just what's needed to reassure you that they are doing well enough. Some Capricorns will be taking a short holiday at the moment and though it is still very early in the year, you could gain from travelling simply to have some fun. Routines could appear somewhat tedious right now.

25 SATURDAY *Moon Age Day 3 Moon Sign Aries*

am ....

pm ....

Social trends are good so that even if you are a Capricorn who works at the weekend there ought to be a few hours during the day to be with people you like and have small adventures. Progress, whilst smooth today, might seem somewhat slow but that won't really matter if you are simply chasing a good time.

26 SUNDAY *Moon Age Day 4 Moon Sign Aries*

am ....

pm ....

You may choose to have a restful Sunday but it is more likely that things simply turn out that way. Enjoy the ride because life can be fun now. The focus is likely to be on leisure and on the state of your love life. You do have confidence to do the right things but could be deliberately delaying action in some cases.

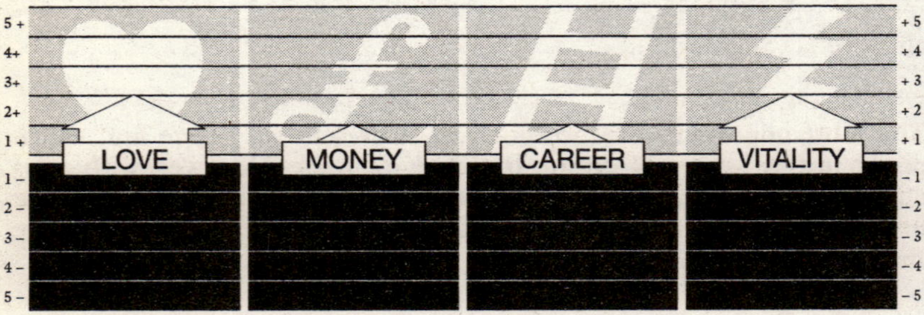

27 MONDAY *Moon Age Day 5 Moon Sign Taurus*

am ....

pm ....

Getting to grips with a work-based issue could find you consulting a number of different useful people. You have mental energy in abundance at present, together with a desire to solve puzzles of one sort or another. These need not be taken from a book but probably relate to life itself.

28 TUESDAY *Moon Age Day 6 Moon Sign Taurus*

am ....

pm ....

There are many interesting messages around at present, some of them coming from people you don't know very well. Rely heavily on your intuition. Don't take your own practical abilities for granted. Issues need some careful thought at the moment otherwise you could find yourself coming slightly unstuck.

29 WEDNESDAY *Moon Age Day 7 Moon Sign Taurus*

am ....

pm ....

There are many advantages on offer, not least of all those that come from knowing that the people you care for the most are doing all they can to lend a hand. You can afford to be really ambitious at the moment and won't be inclined to show the slightly pessimistic streak that Capricorn sometimes displays.

1 THURSDAY *Moon Age Day 8 Moon Sign Gemini*

am ....

pm ....

With plenty going your way and life looking pretty good, you will be feeling fine and able to deal with just about any challenge that comes your way. Keep a sense of proportion over small financial losses. This is a beneficial phase during which you should bring your communication skills to the fore.

2 FRIDAY *Moon Age Day 9 Moon Sign Gemini*

am ....

pm ....

Confidence is growing to say and do the right thing, though it's unlikely you will get on well with absolutely everyone now. What happens today in personal relationships could turn out to be very significant. Others are looking at you positively, and there may be romantic offers from the most unexpected directions.

3 SATURDAY *Moon Age Day 10 Moon Sign Cancer*

am ....

pm ....

Make as much time as possible for relaxation and don't push yourself so hard you find it difficult to slow your mind down later. There is time to do almost anything you want but taking on half a dozen jobs at the same time won't help. A good day for romance, that is if you have the time to notice that you are being observed.

4 SUNDAY *Moon Age Day 11 Moon Sign Cancer*

am ....

pm ....

Be careful not to become involved in small accidents around the home. Rules and regulations could get on your nerves at this time, but remember that some of them are necessary. There are some people around now who are clearly not to be trusted. If you can't stay away from them, treat them with great respect.

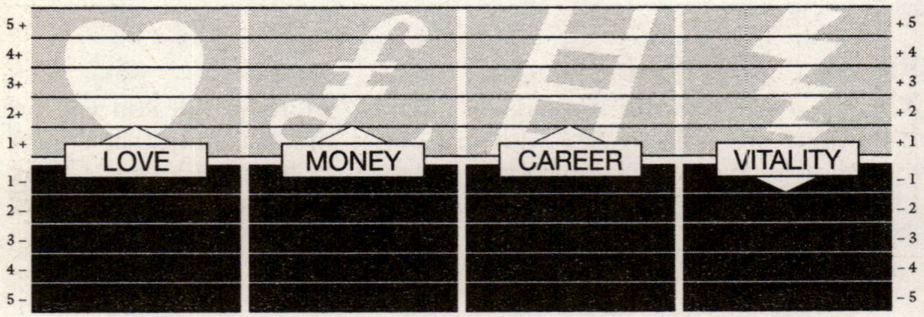

March 2012

Your Month at a Glance

(+) = Opportunities are around (−) = Be on the defensive (●) = Life is pretty ordinary

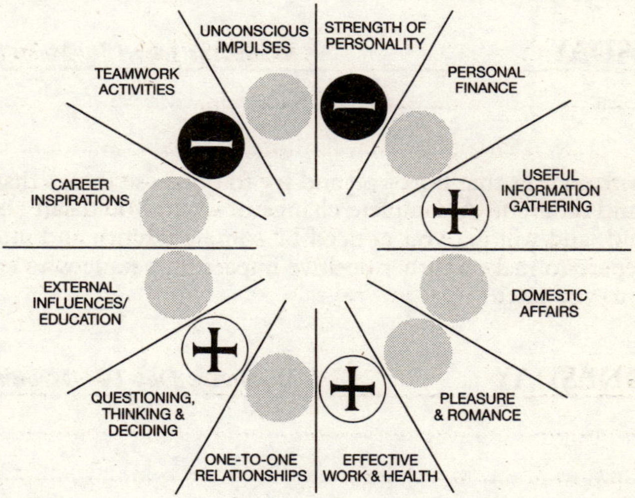

March Highs and Lows

Here I show you how the rhythms of the Moon will affect you this month. Like the tide, your energies and abilities will rise and fall with its pattern. When it is above the centre line, go for it, when it is below, you should be resting.

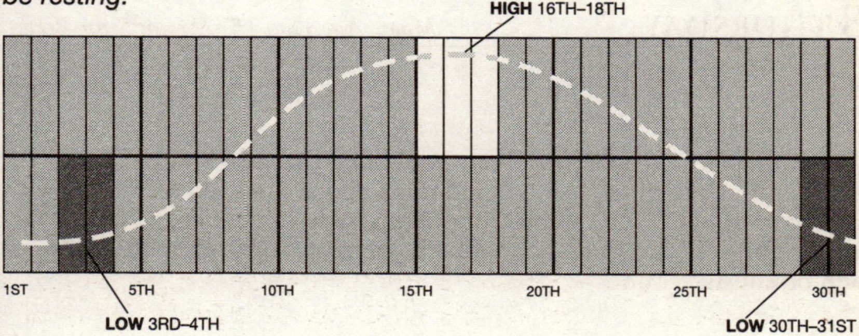

5 MONDAY *Moon Age Day 12 Moon Sign Leo*

am ....

pm ....

This is likely to be a busy month for you, so take any opportunity over the next few days to spend more time with family members, since you won't have much time later. The accent is now on the domestic scene so you should turn your attention towards personal matters associated with house and home.

6 TUESDAY *Moon Age Day 13 Moon Sign Leo*

am ....

pm ....

Stay away from jobs that bore you and try to do those things that can be exciting and different. A complete change of scene would suit you down the ground, and will get you noticed by some attractive and interesting types. Prepare to make a rather positive impact on people who can be of great use to you later.

7 WEDNESDAY *Moon Age Day 14 Moon Sign Leo*

am ....

pm ....

It looks as though you are in a very positive frame of mind today and stand a chance of making a good deal more progress as a result. What might be even more important is your ability to turn heads and to make other people notice the fact that you are around. This can help you in a work sense but also personally.

8 THURSDAY *Moon Age Day 15 Moon Sign Virgo*

am ....

pm ....

Where friends are concerned, you should find that you are the flavour of the month. Take all tasks slowly and think about what you are doing, as a Capricorn should. You can make money in some surprising and ingenious ways right now. Items associated with the past, together with anything odd or unusual count.

9 FRIDAY *Moon Age Day 16 Moon Sign Virgo*

am ....

pm..

Now you push ahead thanks to the natural determination of the zodiac sign of Capricorn. Although this is still a favourable time for you, the full influence of positive planetary aspects fades a little by the middle of the day. As a result, you could find yourself facing what look like difficult odds. This is no time to falter.

10 SATURDAY *Moon Age Day 17 Moon Sign Libra*

am ....

pm..

If you have to work today it's a pity because now you really do want to have fun. Even if you are tied down by responsibility through the day, try to redress the balance in the evening. You should make this one of the most pleasurable days of the month as far as social matters are concerned.

11 SUNDAY *Moon Age Day 18 Moon Sign Libra*

am ....

pm..

You may be happiest today when taking something of a back seat. Letting other people have their head now and again is no bad thing. Besides, you have an ulterior motive. If you make yourself look less than capable, especially at home, someone will come along and do some of the jobs you haven't been looking forward to.

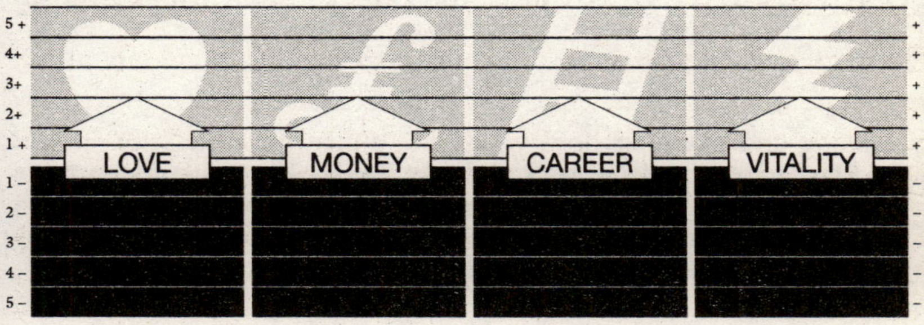

12 MONDAY ☿ *Moon Age Day 19 Moon Sign Scorpio*

am..

pm..

Pay attention because discussions, particularly with loved ones, can be much more important than you might have previously thought. In one or two respects, you may feel you lack courage at present. The fact that you carry on, even though you might be nervous about doing so, proves that you are actually brave.

13 TUESDAY ☿ *Moon Age Day 20 Moon Sign Scorpio*

am..

pm..

Allow the truly inspirational qualities of Capricorn to shine through. More than ever today you can discover that much of what you were worrying about earlier fails to manifest itself at all. Allow this realisation to enhance your confidence and make you far more willing to push towards objectives you know to be possible.

14 WEDNESDAY ☿ *Moon Age Day 21 Moon Sign Sagittarius*

am..

pm..

Your powers of communication are good at present and you can really make an impression when it counts the most. Don't be too quick to judge the wisdom of friends. There are a few possible gains to be made today, some of which come as a surprise. This means you have to be ready for almost anything.

15 THURSDAY ☿ *Moon Age Day 22 Moon Sign Sagittarius*

am..

pm..

By looking and planning now, you make difficult eventualities far less likely. Maybe you should sit back and take a look at your life for an hour or two today. It isn't that anything is going wrong, merely that all sorts of new opportunities wait around the corner and you won't want to miss any of them.

16 FRIDAY ☿ *Moon Age Day 23 Moon Sign Capricorn*

am ....

pm ....

Acting on impulse comes as second nature now that the lunar high is around again. This is the time of the month when you should be actively seeking the chance to make an impression. You can afford to be fairly generous, both with your money and your time, and make a splash at social gatherings.

17 SATURDAY ☿ *Moon Age Day 24 Moon Sign Capricorn*

am ....

pm ....

Prepare yourself for a busy and inspiring interlude. Some of your heart's desires are there to be fulfilled, just as long as you have good vision and show yourself willing to take the odd chance. Nothing was ever achieved in life without taking some sort of risk, and in your case, they are always carefully calculated in any event.

18 SUNDAY ☿ *Moon Age Day 25 Moon Sign Capricorn*

am ....

pm ....

You could be frustrated by a slow start to the day full of idle chatter, so avoid the problem by being up and about early, and stride down to the shops, or even up a mountain! Physical activity appeals to you at the moment and even if you tire yourself out, you will feel that you have genuinely achieved something.

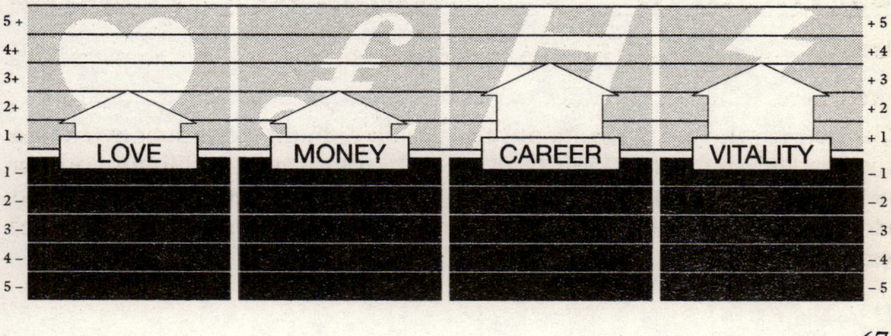

19 MONDAY ☿ *Moon Age Day 26 Moon Sign Aquarius*

am ....

pm ....

Things might quieten down somewhat for today and tomorrow, but that doesn't mean you should stop taking notice of what is going on around you. On the contrary, you really are keeping your eyes open and details that others don't see are immediately obvious to you. Don't be too rash with money right now.

20 TUESDAY ☿ *Moon Age Day 27 Moon Sign Aquarius*

am ....

pm ....

Things that are old, curious or somehow mysterious could have special appeal now, so since this is a day to concentrate on matters of particular interest, an antiques fair or art gallery could be where to go. If you can take others along with you, then so much the better, but what is really important is your own sense of satisfaction.

21 WEDNESDAY ☿ *Moon Age Day 28 Moon Sign Pisces*

am ....

pm ....

Although you can be a good public speaker, there is a slightly shy side to your nature on occasions and you have to overcome this now. Try not to fuss too much about details, as this is one of the less than perfect traits of your sign. If you find yourself facing some sort of social engagement, it would be best to prepare yourself fully first.

22 THURSDAY ☿ *Moon Age Day 0 Moon Sign Pisces*

am ....

pm ....

Capricorns who are not romantically attached should keep their eyes open for new meetings now. Don't put off until tomorrow something you can perfectly well do today. Time seems to stretch like elastic, allowing you to get a lot done, and yet still leaving hours to spend in social pursuits, or with your partner.

23 FRIDAY ☿ *Moon Age Day 1 Moon Sign Aries*

am ....

pm ....

There are obstacles being placed in your path, though few of them are being deliberately created. The secret is to push on regardless and to remain optimistic. Although you are probably feeling generally good about life, it is unlikely that you can make the general headway you would wish at present.

24 SATURDAY ☿ *Moon Age Day 2 Moon Sign Aries*

am ....

pm ....

Picking from what seems like a whole variety of different possibilities, you tend to favour social projects above professional ones right now. Personal relationships ought to be working out especially well. Make this evening a time to remember. This can be an extremely entertaining and positive sort of Saturday.

25 SUNDAY ☿ *Moon Age Day 3 Moon Sign Taurus*

am ....

pm ....

This is potentially a day of social happenings, and a period when you will not want to be tied down by too many routines. Your garden may be of special interest now, or perhaps open land or countryside, even somewhere far from where you live. Don't be too quick to jump to conclusions. There probably isn't too much time for thinking in any case.

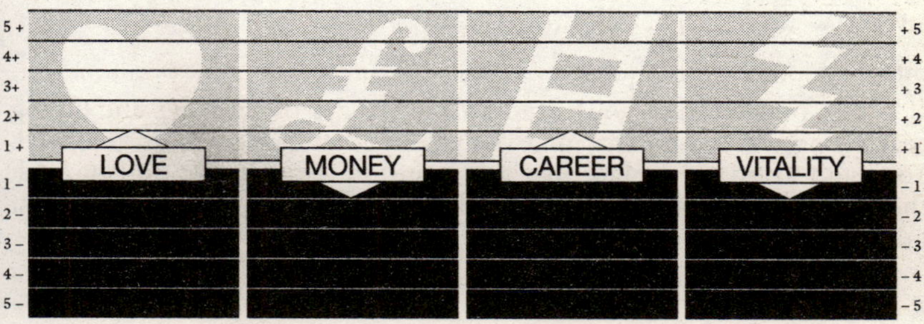

26 MONDAY ☿ *Moon Age Day 4 Moon Sign Taurus*

am..

pm..

You need to speak your mind, especially to your partner, and particularly when you have something good to say. Nobody is going to be in the least embarrassed by your behaviour now, but you may feel this is an unusual approach for you. There are planetary aspects around now that favour a slightly rasher approach, particularly in terms of love and romance.

27 TUESDAY ☿ *Moon Age Day 5 Moon Sign Taurus*

am..

pm..

Friendship is strong and people who have not played an important part in your life up to now start to become more significant. Look out for some unexpected financial gains. There is a chance today to broaden your personal horizons and to get on side with issues that might have puzzled you previously.

28 WEDNESDAY ☿ *Moon Age Day 6 Moon Sign Gemini*

am..

pm..

There are some fairly unusual circumstances about, leading to many coincidences and strange happenings. Most of these seem geared towards your greater success. Make this a good day for new input and ideas, some of which can really bring gains into your life in the fullness of time.

29 THURSDAY ☿ *Moon Age Day 7 Moon Sign Gemini*

am..

pm..

It is just possible that you could abandon ways of thinking and acting that are not yet redundant, in favour of ones that don't serve you as well. You can't avoid the feeling that this is an 'off with the old and on with the new' time in your life generally. That's fine, but don't go too far just because you are on a roll.

30 FRIDAY ☿ *Moon Age Day 8 Moon Sign Cancer*

am ....

pm ....

It could seem as if you do nothing but wait today. Not to worry, the lunar low is around in any case, so you won't be able to move any mountains. You have time to think and the ability to structure your thoughts into patterns of behaviour that will be far more appropriate on another day.

31 SATURDAY ☿ *Moon Age Day 9 Moon Sign Cancer*

am ....

pm ....

Today is best spent planning, and observing the way others do things. You need these periods of calm and quiet in order to deal with the busier times that crop up regularly this year. The practical side of your nature is in evidence, but unless you are really sure about what you are doing, leave it until later.

1 SUNDAY ☿ *Moon Age Day 10 Moon Sign Cancer*

am ....

pm ....

April arrives, and if you choose to play the April Fool with anyone today, it is likely to be only on yourself. To others, you appear confident, able to address all type of issues and willing to make compromises where necessary. Don't be too quick to judge the rather puzzling behaviour of a good friend.

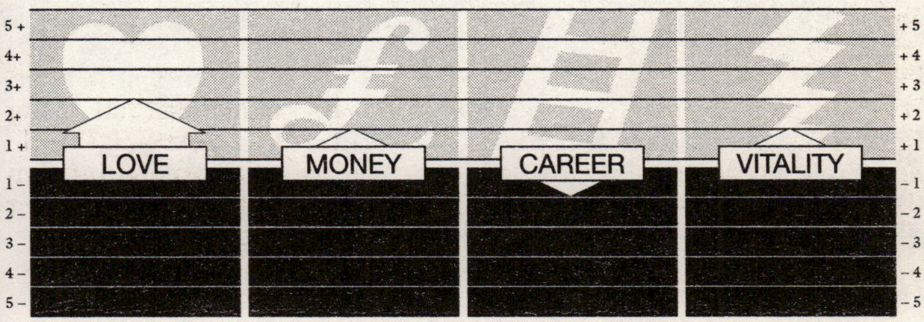

April

2012

Your Month at a Glance

⊕ = Opportunities are around ⊖ = Be on the defensive ● = Life is pretty ordinary

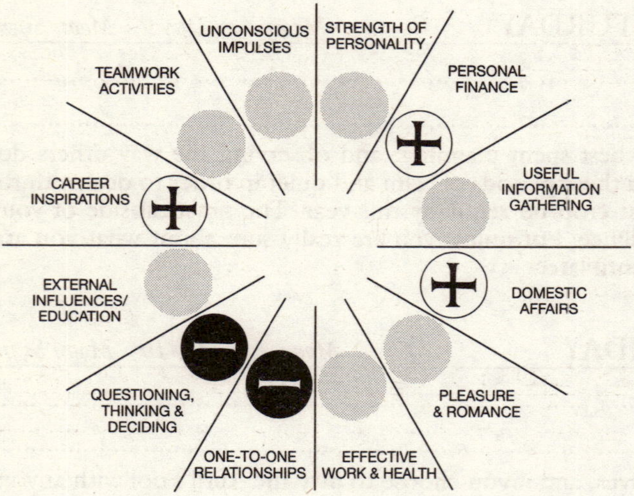

April Highs and Lows

Here I show you how the rhythms of the Moon will affect you this month. Like the tide, your energies and abilities will rise and fall with its pattern. When it is above the centre line, go for it, when it is below, you should be resting.

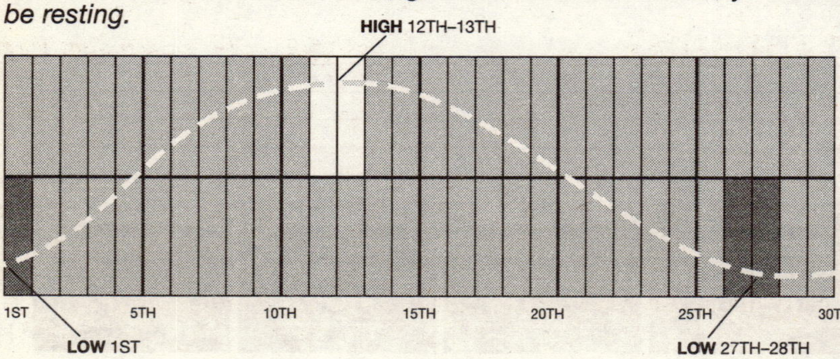

2 MONDAY ☿ *Moon Age Day 11 Moon Sign Leo*

am ....

pm ....

Taking life in your stride, you should enjoy today and are likely to be making a great many personal offers and invitations. When it comes to romance, you are in a good position to show your lover exactly how you feel. Impressive socially, get out there because the world has some enjoyable and stimulating company for you.

3 TUESDAY ☿ *Moon Age Day 12 Moon Sign Leo*

am ....

pm ....

In an everyday sense it would be sensible to avoid putting off until tomorrow what you can easily do today. People you haven't met for ages are likely to make a return to your life now. A less interesting period might seem to be in evidence, following the generally positive astrological trends of yesterday.

4 WEDNESDAY ☿ *Moon Age Day 13 Moon Sign Virgo*

am ....

pm ....

There are gains to be made now through inventiveness and by being in the right place at the most advantageous time. Where emotional ties are concerned, you need to be rather more careful than usual. It is easy for others to misunderstand what you are saying and to come to the wrong conclusions as a result.

5 THURSDAY *Moon Age Day 14 Moon Sign Virgo*

am ....

pm ....

You can be very stubborn when you feel you are being browbeaten and this is certainly no time to follow pointless instructions. Those who understand you best will not be particularly surprised by your attitude. Doing your own thing is the way forward for you now, rather than toeing a party line in any situation.

6 FRIDAY *Moon Age Day 15 Moon Sign Libra*

am ....

pm ....

Venus is now in a strong position for you, so it would be wise not to disclose some of your most favoured ambitions, but you ought to know automatically who you can afford to talk to with confidence. Maybe you could be a little more ambitious and even dominating in certain areas of your life?

7 SATURDAY *Moon Age Day 16 Moon Sign Libra*

am ....

pm ....

Remain interested and flexible today, but only up to a point. Don't allow the views of others to influence your own life to any great degree today. Of course, it is important to take on board alternative opinions, but that isn't the same as turning your world upside-down to accommodate them.

8 SUNDAY *Moon Age Day 17 Moon Sign Scorpio*

am ....

pm ....

People are generally on your side, even if it doesn't always appear that this is the case. A few emotional tensions can begin to surface now, which could leave you feeling slightly wrung out. Although these have to be addressed, perhaps you don't have to take them quite as seriously as you may think.

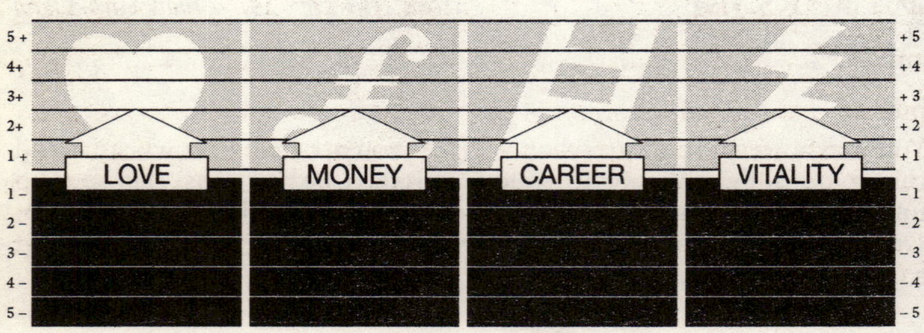

9 MONDAY *Moon Age Day 18 Moon Sign Scorpio*

am ....

pm ....

The summer is approaching fast, with the nights getting shorter and everything in the garden beginning to grow. Like the flowers, you need more space now. When it comes to general initiative, you won't be found in any way wanting on this Monday. At the same time, you do need to take a close look around you.

10 TUESDAY *Moon Age Day 19 Moon Sign Sagittarius*

am ....

pm ....

Don't be too quick to make widespread changes to domestic arrangements, at least without bearing in mind the opinions of family members. Professional matters seem to be on a very definite roll, making you increasingly confident about situations, a fact that shows in the way you deal with them.

11 WEDNESDAY *Moon Age Day 20 Moon Sign Sagittarius*

am ....

pm ....

Congratulations may be in order somewhere in the family or amongst your dearest friends. You will be the first to make a fuss of the people concerned and to show your joy. The dynamism to get things done in a practical sense is strong, reconfirming your belief that you are doing the right things at the right time.

12 THURSDAY *Moon Age Day 21 Moon Sign Capricorn*

am ....

pm ....

You can't have everything you want from life at present, though you can come quite close. Lady Luck is with you and it's worth investing in what you know to be a good idea, especially if you thought it up for yourself. Speak your mind today, and expect everyone to give you their full attention.

13 FRIDAY *Moon Age Day 22 Moon Sign Capricorn*

am ....

pm ....

This is another excellent time for putting your luck to the test. Progressive decision-making is also possible, together with a strong sense of destiny regarding specific issues. Elements of the past have a bearing on the present and there may be a significant amount of coincidences cropping up around now.

14 SATURDAY *Moon Age Day 23 Moon Sign Aquarius*

am ....

pm ....

Casual conversations lead to ideas that can prove to be both interesting and useful. Look out for unusual happenings that start you thinking along unconventional lines. Personal relationships can be a great deal of help today when it comes to financial support and future planning of a practical nature.

15 SUNDAY *Moon Age Day 24 Moon Sign Aquarius*

am ....

pm ....

Exercise some caution if you are faced by get-rich-quick schemes. If they look too good to be true, they probably are. Certain situations can seem fairly chaotic today, particularly in terms of necessary communication. Actually, you will probably be far better off spending some time alone and relying on your own intuition.

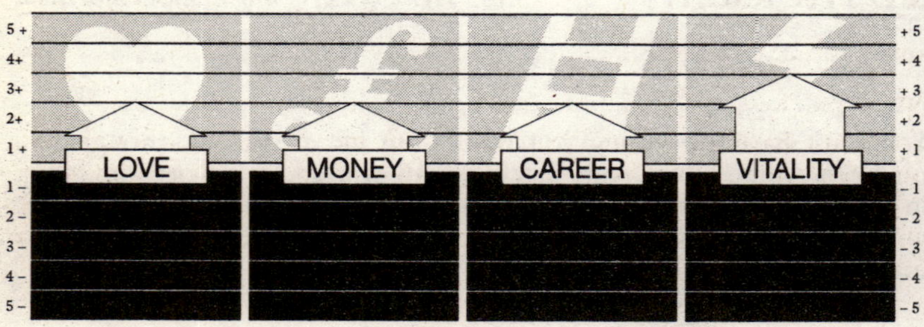

16 MONDAY *Moon Age Day 25 Moon Sign Aquarius*

am ....

pm ....

Keep active and don't allow yourself to vegetate. It is only a matter of time before new and stimulating situations begin, though today is unlikely to be bristling with them. It appears that you need a change from your everyday routines and the start of a new working week could offer all the incentive you need.

17 TUESDAY *Moon Age Day 26 Moon Sign Pisces*

am ....

pm ....

In matters of the heart you should be frank and outspoken but be careful you are not a little brutal on occasions. It isn't sensible to believe everything you hear today. The fact is that there are people about who are fairly deceptive. Stay away from them if you can, but if not, use your intuition and caution.

18 WEDNESDAY *Moon Age Day 27 Moon Sign Pisces*

am ....

pm ....

It is time to enjoy the fruits of some of your recent efforts. Financially speaking you could be rather better off than you have been expecting and the world looks more exciting than for some days past. You are right to be confident in your own abilities. All in all, you should be looking and feeling good.

19 THURSDAY *Moon Age Day 28 Moon Sign Aries*

am ....

pm ....

There are certain issues that would be best left on the back burner for the moment, leaving you to have fun and to look at life in a more light-hearted way. A rather pressing domestic matter could arise today. Take it in your stride and don't necessarily think that you have to find answers here and now.

20 FRIDAY *Moon Age Day 29 Moon Sign Aries*

am ....

pm ....

Although you are still very committed to change, you should also recognise how important it is to think carefully before you act. Show a very sensible face to the world today, then you will strike a balance between self-interest and what is required of you.

21 SATURDAY *Moon Age Day 0 Moon Sign Aries*

am ....

pm ....

Confidence remains essentially high so you should look with some certainty at plans to revolutionise your professional life. Domestic obligations might hamper your efforts to get ahead in the outside world. If they do, accept that this is only a very temporary situation and avoid any temptation to overreact.

22 SUNDAY *Moon Age Day 1 Moon Sign Taurus*

am ....

pm ....

Along comes a period when you will delight in the opportunity to get out and about. There are things to do and people to meet. The sociable side of your nature is more than evident and you will enjoy all sorts of company. Don't be surprised if you find yourself on the receiving end of someone's joke.

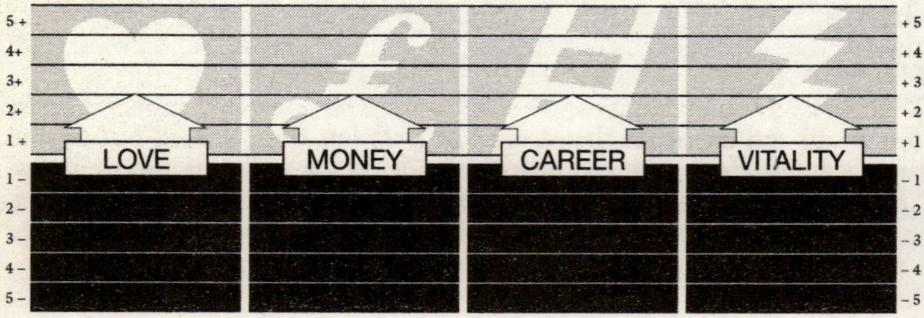

23 MONDAY *Moon Age Day 2 Moon Sign Taurus*

am ....

pm ....

There is now much to be gained from widening your personal horizons. Young Capricorns, or those looking for love, can look out for opportunities coming along. Maybe you have a secret admirer you would never have guessed, or perhaps you discover that a friend would wish to be very much more.

24 TUESDAY *Moon Age Day 3 Moon Sign Gemini*

am ....

pm ....

Your personal life is likely to be settled, with romantic interludes permeating a generally sedate period. The potential for making smooth progress is strong. At work, you should be able to address most matters well and not need to back down over issues you see as being important.

25 WEDNESDAY *Moon Age Day 4 Moon Sign Gemini*

am ....

pm ....

Your nature is now rock solid, causing others to have a deep and abiding confidence in your decisions. The fact that this appears to place an extra burden on you is something you don't recognise at all. You know the value of self-reliance and can easily go your own way. This is particularly true today.

26 THURSDAY *Moon Age Day 5 Moon Sign Gemini*

am ....

pm ....

You are likely to be happiest when amongst those you love at this end of the week, and particularly today. It isn't that you feel threatened by the outside world but it will be most advantageous to focus on domestic issues. Your home is your castle and for the moment, keeping the drawbridge up is the best idea.

27 FRIDAY *Moon Age Day 6 Moon Sign Cancer*

am...

pm...

When it comes to obligations, you might want to take life rather easily at present. The lunar low makes you somewhat lethargic and less than happy to push yourself physically. Routines suit you just at the moment because there is great security in doing what you know and understand.

28 SATURDAY *Moon Age Day 7 Moon Sign Cancer*

am...

pm...

Today the real cautious side of your zodiac sign is revealed, causing you to move forward very carefully. Try to resolve any disputes still around in your circle of friends. Where decisions are concerned today, you should show even more circumspection than was necessary yesterday.

29 SUNDAY *Moon Age Day 8 Moon Sign Leo*

am...

pm...

You would do well to look for a number of new ways to get ahead with your work and should also be enjoying the cut and thrust of an active life that could involve colleagues. Family matters might have to be left on the back burner for a short while. It is towards the practical aspects of life that your mind now turns.

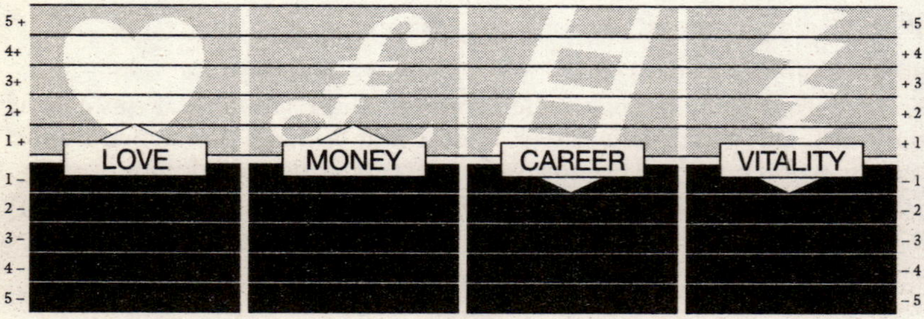

30 MONDAY *Moon Age Day 9 Moon Sign Leo*

am...

pm...

Shopping today could lead to the discovery of genuine bargains, whilst social possibilities look particularly good. If there isn't much happening around you, the chances are you are not trying as hard as you could. There are now great opportunities for gain and ones that you will not want to pass by.

1 TUESDAY *Moon Age Day 10 Moon Sign Virgo*

am...

pm...

It may well benefit you to be a little pushier than has been the case of late. Not everyone is doing what they can to improve situations around you and it is up to you to put them back on track. This will be particularly true if you are a working Capricorn with specific responsibilities.

2 WEDNESDAY *Moon Age Day 11 Moon Sign Virgo*

am...

pm...

Routines are not acceptable to you and you really want to be instinctive and to do what comes naturally in a moment-by-moment sense. Your personal associations with others show just how strong your influence now is. Not only do people want to listen to what you have to say, they almost instinctively follow your lead.

3 THURSDAY *Moon Age Day 12 Moon Sign Libra*

am...

pm...

You are about to realise just how popular and also how capable your sign of Capricorn can be. This may turn out to be one of the best social times of the month and maybe of the year. Stay out there in the social limelight and be prepared to take the lead when others indicate you should do so.

4 FRIDAY *Moon Age Day 13 Moon Sign Libra*

am ....

pm ....

Avoid unnecessary routines and concentrate on those matters you know to be of supreme importance. Keep a sense of proportion over professional matters. This should be an enjoyable time as far as your love life is concerned. You seem to be particularly charming at the moment and can certainly turn heads.

5 SATURDAY *Moon Age Day 14 Moon Sign Scorpio*

am ....

pm ....

Someone you haven't seen for a long time may be paying a return visit to your life and they are likely to bring interesting possibilities with them. Conforming to domestic expectations could be slightly more difficult. There is a little more difficulty today when it comes to concentrating on specific efforts.

6 SUNDAY *Moon Age Day 15 Moon Sign Scorpio*

am ....

pm ....

Stand up for someone who you think is going through a bad time and argue their corner with all the tenacity of which your zodiac sign is capable. In a monetary sense you are now in a position to get ahead. This probably has to do with your efforts over the last few months and is not an immediate matter.

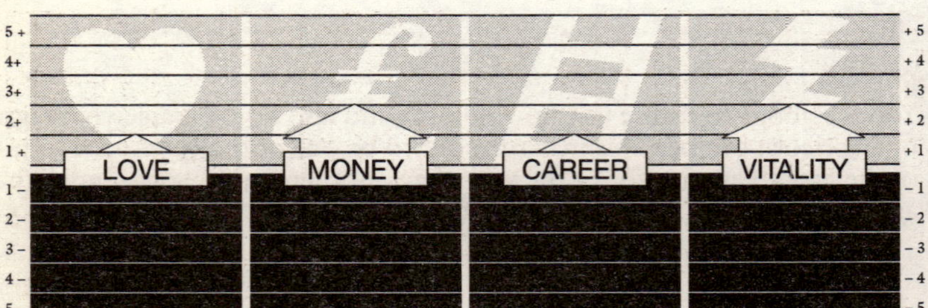

May

2012

Your Month at a Glance

(+) = Opportunities are around (–) = Be on the defensive (●) = Life is pretty ordinary

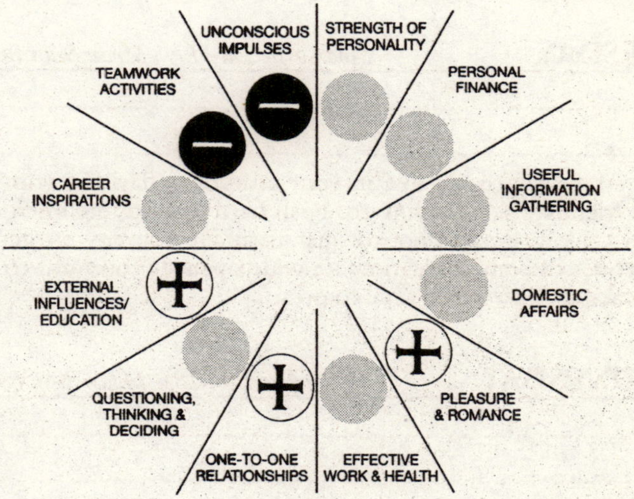

May Highs and Lows

Here I show you how the rhythms of the Moon will affect you this month. Like the tide, your energies and abilities will rise and fall with its pattern. When it is above the centre line, go for it, when it is below, you should be resting.

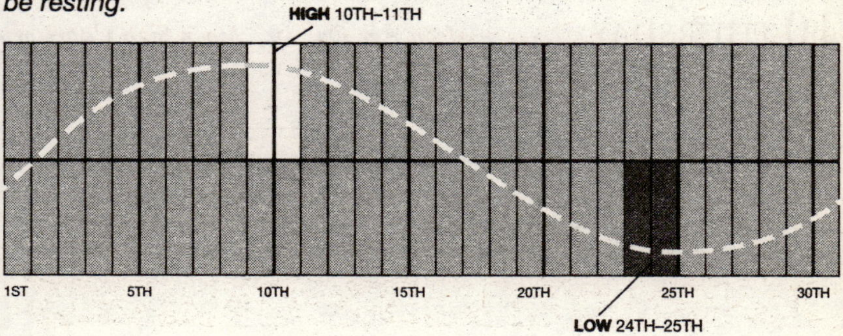

7 MONDAY *Moon Age Day 16 Moon Sign Scorpio*

am ....

pm ....

At the moment you are likely to disagree openly with people whose attitudes you don't care for. It is often the case that Capricorn keeps its counsel but present trends show that you are more inclined to speak out now. Look for some real personalities entering your life and make the most of their refreshing presence.

8 TUESDAY *Moon Age Day 17 Moon Sign Sagittarius*

am ....

pm ....

Remain essentially reasonable in your attitude today and you will tend to make friends wherever you go. Push hard towards a chosen objective and don't allow those who are just naturally grumpy to get in your way. Avenues of communication are wide open. If you want to get your message across, now is the time to do so.

9 WEDNESDAY *Moon Age Day 18 Moon Sign Sagittarius*

am ....

pm ....

You will find your friends are supportive and kind when you need them, the more so as the day advances. You ought to be happily on the go today but won't be able to make quite the headway you would wish. As a result, you will probably turn your attention toward relationships, which could have taken a background position of late.

10 THURSDAY *Moon Age Day 19 Moon Sign Capricorn*

am ....

pm ....

You can afford to take the odd chance as you discover that general luck is on your side. People are showing great faith in your abilities and it looks as though you now have great confidence in yourself. The lunar high merely emphasises a whole host of positive trends that surround you at present.

11 FRIDAY *Moon Age Day 20 Moon Sign Capricorn*

am ....

pm ....

If there isn't quite enough time to spend with loved ones today, they should realise this and be likely to bolster your attempts to get ahead. Busy you may be, but you are also quite charming. This is a time of great energy, with very little rest and a determination to see plans through to their logical conclusion.

12 SATURDAY *Moon Age Day 21 Moon Sign Aquarius*

am ....

pm ....

Consideration for others is still strong and the social conscience of Capricorn has rarely been more marked. The attitude of a particular friend might be somewhat strange and a little gentle digging is called for to establish why. You should tap into the fact that this is likely to be a very upbeat phase in terms of your overall energy.

13 SUNDAY *Moon Age Day 22 Moon Sign Aquarius*

am ....

pm ....

Normal events keep you pretty much on the move, so you can forget today as being a day of rest. But you should have enough energy to rush about from one task to another. In amongst all the jobs you take on, social trends are also good so find time to mix freely.

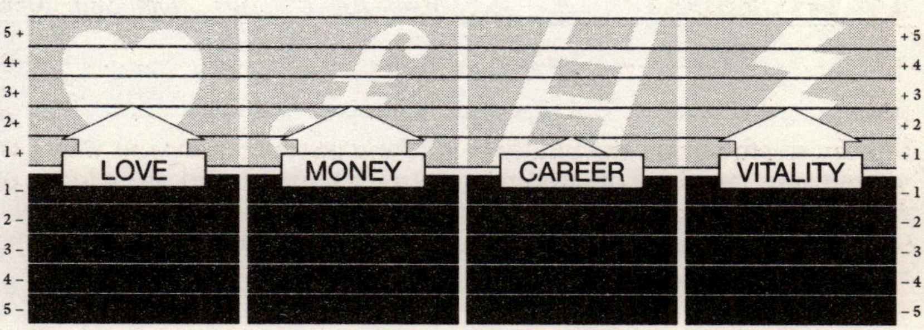

14 MONDAY *Moon Age Day 23 Moon Sign Pisces*

am ....

pm..

Now ingenious and positive, you can make a tremendous impression on the world if you make the effort. There may be some problems arising now from money, or perhaps the lack of it. This is not something to stop you in your tracks. On the contrary, use it to inspire your fantastic Capricorn ability to make do.

15 TUESDAY *Moon Age Day 24 Moon Sign Pisces*

am ....

pm..

Some uncertainty is more or less inevitable right now but such is your present strength of character, you can plough through small difficulties with ease. Although trends suggest that you are clearly attracting life's little luxuries at this time, you may find the price you have to pay in order to get them rather high.

16 WEDNESDAY *Moon Age Day 25 Moon Sign Aries*

am ....

pm..

This would be an excellent time for travel and holidays and also for making major changes to your professional life. In a domestic context, many Capricorns will now be either thinking about making changes at home or perhaps moving home. This is a good time to show your independent and even adventurous spirit.

17 THURSDAY *Moon Age Day 26 Moon Sign Aries*

am ....

pm..

You are still full of energy and there is very little to stand in your way. Use your strong creative potential to good effect to forward all manner of new activities. There are some unusual circumstances today, particularly a series of unexpected coincidences, which could be unsettling but can be turned to your advantage.

18 FRIDAY *Moon Age Day 27 Moon Sign Aries*

am ....

pm..

With plenty to occupy your mind, you are hardly likely to become bored but it is true that a comfortable chair and a good book will look inviting. At last, along comes a period during which you will benefit more from a little peace and quiet than you would from the roller coaster that has been your life recently.

19 SATURDAY *Moon Age Day 28 Moon Sign Taurus*

am ....

pm..

It's off with the old and on with the new today. This is not simply a matter of tidying up your home but also elements of your thinking. Such periods are few and far between for Capricorn so now is the time to dispense with habits and thought patterns that have been holding you back.

20 SUNDAY *Moon Age Day 0 Moon Sign Taurus*

am ....

pm..

This is certainly a period during which you benefit from keeping on the move. The old stick-in-the-mud that Capricorn can be on occasions is nowhere to be seen at this stage of the month. You won't have any real trouble discovering where interesting things are happening, or assessing who is in the know.

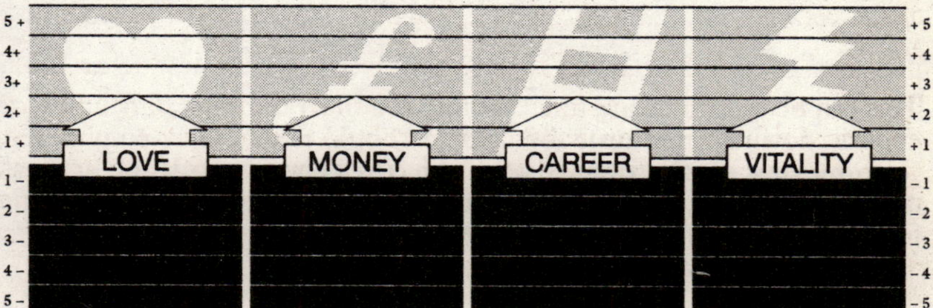

21 MONDAY *Moon Age Day 1 Moon Sign Gemini*

am ....

pm ....

You may feel a desire for fresh fields and pastures new, which is as much a response to the season as to any astrological trend. Try to get away from mundane issues at the start of this week and avoid sticking around your home. You may not feel like it at first but it will be worth the effort.

22 TUESDAY *Moon Age Day 2 Moon Sign Gemini*

am ....

pm ....

It looks as though one-to-one relationships could be the source of some bickering today, though this is completely pointless and you would do yourself a real favour if you refused to be involved. Friendships or working relationships that are less emotionally motivated might offer slightly more for today.

23 WEDNESDAY *Moon Age Day 3 Moon Sign Gemini*

am ....

pm ....

If you are a working Capricorn, there is room for advancement this week or at the very least a promise of it in the not too distant future. Concentrating on matters that don't interest you is likely to be difficult as you are likely to be in a restless frame of mind right now, so why not try out some new proposals.

24 THURSDAY *Moon Age Day 4 Moon Sign Cancer*

am ....

pm ....

This can be quite a taxing time, though the short duration difficulties are entirely down to the lunar low and so should not be over-emphasised. Keep moving slowly towards your objectives and try to laugh at small obstacles that get in your way. You are more than capable of pushing forward all the same.

25 FRIDAY *Moon Age Day 5 Moon Sign Cancer*

am ....

pm..

If you feel your energies are not so strong whilst the lunar low is around, you should still be able to maintain the momentum you have established recently. Treat today in particular as a time when some thought and a little rest are a priority and you won't go far wrong.

26 SATURDAY *Moon Age Day 6 Moon Sign Leo*

am ....

pm..

Looking outward is crucially important if you want to get the best of present planetary trends. If you are quick to act, you can make gains as a direct result of the hesitation of those around you. This is not to imply you are moving ahead at the expense of others because you are also very helpful today.

27 SUNDAY *Moon Age Day 7 Moon Sign Leo*

am ....

pm..

It is true that there can be minor frustrations around at this time, though if you are prepared for them there isn't much of a problem. These will undoubtedly come from the direction of close friends or family members, some of whom are unwilling or unable to follow your present reasoning and so could cause delays.

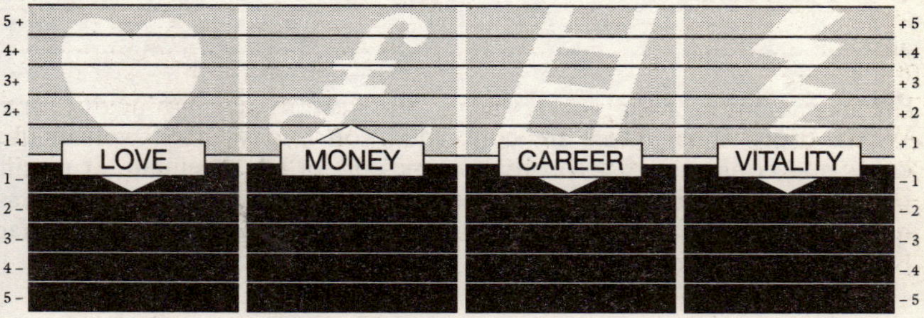

28 MONDAY *Moon Age Day 8 Moon Sign Leo*

am..

pm..

It seems as though your nature is now more forceful and even dominant in some ways. This is the period of the month during which you can definitely get ahead in a practical way. As a result, the needs of your personal life could appear to suffer somewhat, though if you realise that this is the case, you will address the situation.

29 TUESDAY *Moon Age Day 9 Moon Sign Virgo*

am..

pm..

It is clear that Capricorn is in the mood for romance and this trend comes along at a period when your partner probably has the greatest need of you for some time. Mixing business with pleasure should be beneficial. Most professional interactions are harmonious, but not half as much as personal ones.

30 WEDNESDAY *Moon Age Day 10 Moon Sign Virgo*

am..

pm..

The focus today is on creative pursuits and you can gain a great deal if you allow this side of your nature to predominate. There are plenty of hints as to the most profitable way forward today. You should feel free to express yourself and you won't have any trouble at all finding the right words to do so.

31 THURSDAY *Moon Age Day 11 Moon Sign Libra*

am..

pm..

Where professional issues are concerned you find yourself well in the know and could use that to obtain some sort of advancement. It might be that you are being told what to do by people you consider to be less qualified than you are. However, a degree of co-operation will work far better than direct criticism.

1 FRIDAY *Moon Age Day 12 Moon Sign Libra*

am...

pm...

Keep abreast of what is going on in your immediate vicinity with daily encounters with others. You may also feel you want to know more about what is going on in the world outside so watch the television news and scan the newspapers to learn more. Capricorn is very alert now.

2 SATURDAY *Moon Age Day 13 Moon Sign Scorpio*

am...

pm...

You can do much to lift the spirits of a depressed friend at this time. At the same time it may be that others seem a little opinionated at the moment but you really should take a look at yourself. Capricorn can be very definite about its feelings and you might benefit from a little more consideration and a slightly modified attitude.

3 SUNDAY *Moon Age Day 14 Moon Sign Scorpio*

am...

pm...

The more the year advances, the greater is your tendency to seek out new sights and little adventures. Capricorn should be flexing its muscles around this time. A fast pace of events in the social arena can lead to an interesting Sunday and especially so if you are not committed to work right now.

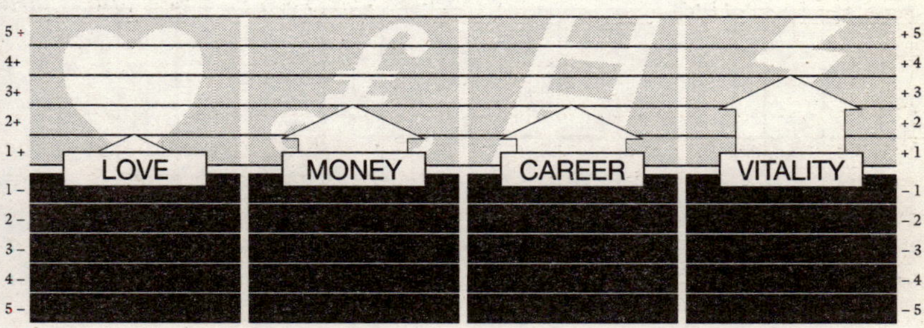

♑

June 2012

Your Month at a Glance

⊕ = Opportunities are around ⊖ = Be on the defensive ● = Life is pretty ordinary

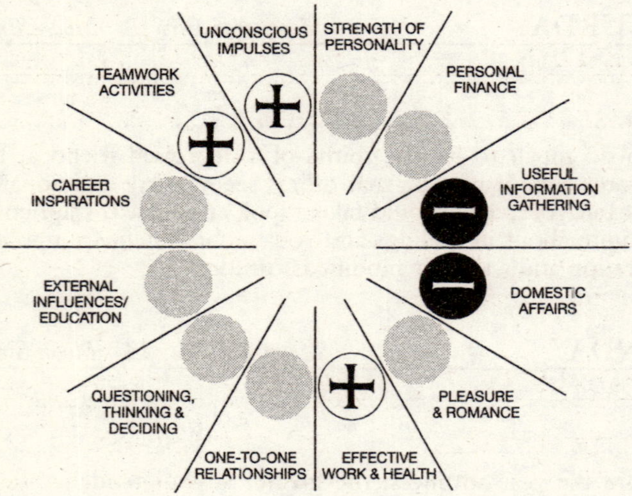

June Highs and Lows

Here I show you how the rhythms of the Moon will affect you this month. Like the tide, your energies and abilities will rise and fall with its pattern. When it is above the centre line, go for it, when it is below, you should be resting.

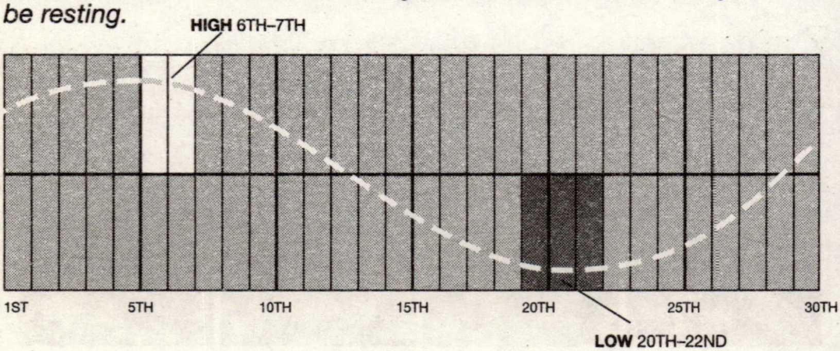

4 MONDAY *Moon Age Day 15 Moon Sign Sagittarius*

am ....

pm ....

Concern for family members could be somewhat premature and it might be sensible to take a generally tolerant point of view if not everyone is behaving in quite the way you have come to expect. This is a good time for showing off and letting others know who you are and what you are capable of.

5 TUESDAY *Moon Age Day 16 Moon Sign Sagittarius*

am ....

pm ....

The Moon is in your solar twelfth house and this can make you slightly introspective. Try to be involved in social activities and maybe go on a shopping spree. A personal or private matter might need more thought but there isn't much point in mulling things over to quite the extent you are likely to do at present.

6 WEDNESDAY *Moon Age Day 17 Moon Sign Capricorn*

am ....

pm ....

There is nothing particularly circumspect about your attitude at this time and it is clear that you are firing on all cylinders. Things should be going your way, leaving you in the right frame of mind to take on new projects and to really get to grips with work matters that have bugged you for a while.

7 THURSDAY *Moon Age Day 18 Moon Sign Capricorn*

am ....

pm ....

Your potential good fortune in the finance department comes mainly through keeping your eye on the ball. The lunar high can be quite useful in this regard, not least because you are on the receiving end of help from friends and acquaintances. Don't miss the chance of a small but fortunate speculation.

8 FRIDAY *Moon Age Day 19 Moon Sign Aquarius*

am ....

pm..

For now, rules and regulations are easy to follow, but may be more difficult where they affect other family members. You may have your work cut out today trying to keep on top of material problems, which is why it would be very sensible to call upon the help and advice of people who are genuinely in the know.

9 SATURDAY *Moon Age Day 20 Moon Sign Aquarius*

am ....

pm..

It has to be stressed that this is an ideal time for brand new work projects and even for getting yourself a completely new job. On a more personal footing, you appear to be making the very best impression on someone for whom you care deeply. Keep happy and smiling because you are clearly being noticed.

10 SUNDAY *Moon Age Day 21 Moon Sign Pisces*

am ....

pm..

You could be in too deep for your own good when assessing romantic attachments. Perhaps you are looking for something that doesn't exist or else deluding yourself in some other way. Beware of certain emotional driving forces at the moment that might lead you off a sensible path and towards difficulties.

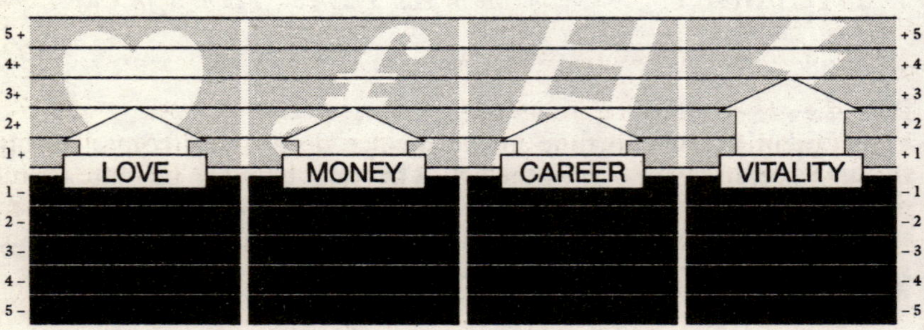

11 MONDAY *Moon Age Day 22 Moon Sign Pisces*

am ....

pm ....

Friends try to be very supportive but it is possible that you only have eyes for one specific person at the moment. Intimate relationships can make life especially rewarding at the start of this week. Include an outing of some sort in your diary as you might find this will be very enjoyable and will offer you the relaxation you need.

12 TUESDAY *Moon Age Day 23 Moon Sign Pisces*

am ....

pm ....

Don't expect to be able to bring everyone round to your particular point of view and watch out for a few slight problems regarding money or travel arrangements. However, you should be doing especially well in a professional sense. For some time now people have been watching you carefully and probably assessing you for new responsibilities.

13 WEDNESDAY *Moon Age Day 24 Moon Sign Aries*

am ....

pm ....

Look out for gains from some quite unexpected directions which could offer you new incentives. Friends should prove to be both helpful and interested in what you have to say. You ought to be getting where you want to go in several senses now but certainly with regard to work.

14 THURSDAY *Moon Age Day 25 Moon Sign Aries*

am ....

pm ....

Take the opportunity to be sociable today, which is a positive fact for a number of different reasons. In addition to making other people feel good, you also have the possibility of feathering your own nest in ways you never intended. You should also find more in the way of general good luck coming along.

15 FRIDAY *Moon Age Day 26 Moon Sign Taurus*

am ....

pm...

No matter how well you plan things today there is a slight threat of confusion being the result. This is not directly as a result of your own actions but you can work against the tendency by being particularly careful. Another way of dealing with this trend is to push ideas and schemes back a day.

16 SATURDAY *Moon Age Day 27 Moon Sign Taurus*

am ....

pm...

Everyone needs to have fun now and again and it is your time today and tomorrow. You have a great chance to increase your circle of close friends over the next couple of days. Although if you tried you could make even more progress in a practical or a professional sense, enough may be enough for the moment.

17 SUNDAY *Moon Age Day 28 Moon Sign Taurus*

am ....

pm...

A positive and forward-looking response to most situations is what you require and can find. Today finds you showing a generally optimistic attitude regarding matters that could have caused you some concern in the recent past. Whilst you are in this frame of mind you seem to have the ability to show the world how capable you are.

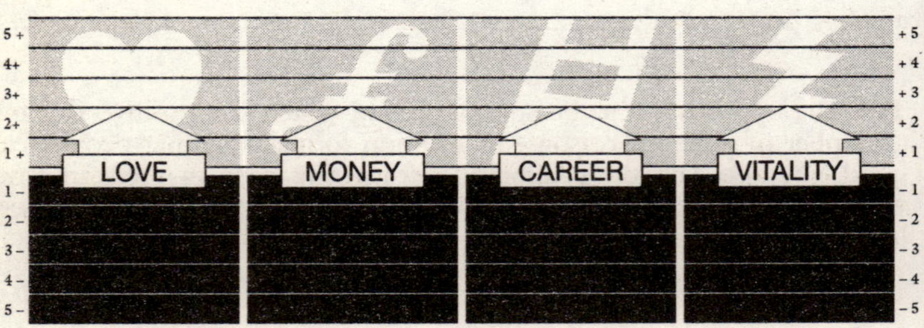

18 MONDAY *Moon Age Day 29 Moon Sign Gemini*

am..

pm..

Although you usually have the ability to do more than one thing at once, this skill seems to be somewhat lacking right now. Try to get yourself involved in projects today that need to be finished before you start others. You will probably have more influence today with people who are especially important to your life.

19 TUESDAY *Moon Age Day 0 Moon Sign Gemini*

am..

pm..

Capricorn is one of the most capable of all the zodiac signs, even if it sometimes takes itself rather too seriously. This certainly isn't the case under present trends. The recognition that others have of your abilities is not in doubt at present, which is why you can make such an impression on them.

20 WEDNESDAY *Moon Age Day 1 Moon Sign Cancer*

am..

pm..

There are more or less inevitable hold-ups today. If you are wise you will realise that this is not the best time for starting new projects or for trying to bulldoze your way towards chosen objectives. Take a day or two to think about things and whilst you are doing so, enjoy the positive domestic and personal trends.

21 THURSDAY *Moon Age Day 2 Moon Sign Cancer*

am..

pm..

It will appear to you that your partner, or maybe someone you are especially fond of, is behaving in a less than rational way but maybe you should also look in the mirror. Relationships generally could be at quite a low ebb on occasions today and this is especially true in the case of romantic attachments.

22 FRIDAY *Moon Age Day 3 Moon Sign Cancer*

am ....

pm ....

Today is a better day to concentrate on love and also to make a startling impression on people who can have an important part to play in your life in the months to come. You easily express charm, grace and harmony at the moment, so there is no wonder that you are wowing almost everyone you come across.

23 SATURDAY *Moon Age Day 4 Moon Sign Leo*

am ....

pm ....

If you are at work today, look out for very rewarding situations, mainly because of the effort you put in. Things are likely to be rather hectic today and there won't be too much time to catch your breath. To a great extent you have to rely on your intuition and on the advice of specific people who you know to have your best interests at heart.

24 SUNDAY *Moon Age Day 5 Moon Sign Leo*

am ....

pm ....

In between finding excellent ways to enjoy yourself, it is clear that you should be casting your mind into the future and coming up with some cracking schemes. You will almost certainly have good ideas now for improving work-based problems or situations, whether or not you are actually at work today.

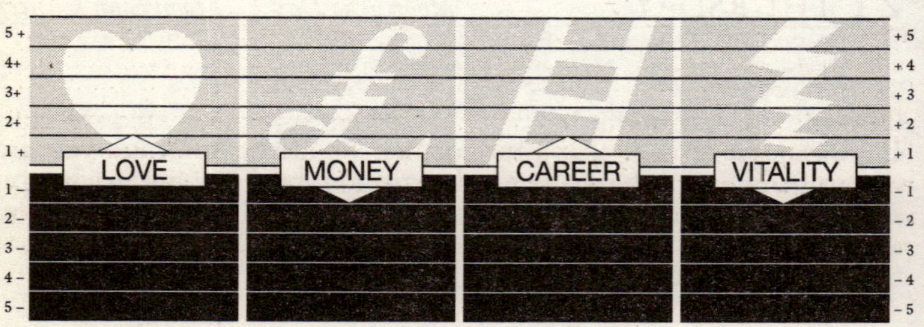

25 MONDAY *Moon Age Day 6 Moon Sign Virgo*

am ....

pm ....

There is plenty of room for romance in your life at present and it appears that you should be taking the time to show your partner, or someone you really fancy, how very kind you can be. There is likely to be some hopeful news arriving regarding situations that might not appear to have been working out well for you recently.

26 TUESDAY *Moon Age Day 7 Moon Sign Virgo*

am ....

pm ....

Whether in business or pleasure, twosomes work especially well for you and co-operative ventures of any sort are now much more likely to turn out well. A more than favourable period is coming along, especially with regard to relationships, which look particularly settled around this time.

27 WEDNESDAY *Moon Age Day 8 Moon Sign Libra*

am ....

pm ....

Your social and love life is likely to be very fulfilling around now and you won't have any problem at all getting others to join in the fun you are instigating. You ought to find yourself in amongst just the right company today and are able to make the most positive of impressions when it counts the most.

28 THURSDAY *Moon Age Day 9 Moon Sign Libra*

am ....

pm ....

Although you may not be letting your hair down big-time, and will still be showing some caution, you have powerful social inclinations now and want to share your opinions with others. A short journey might suit you well. The ability to get along well and easily with others is now very strong indeed.

29 FRIDAY *Moon Age Day 10 Moon Sign Scorpio*

am ....

pm..

Don't be at all surprised if a number of quite significant invitations are coming your way during the next couple of days. Popularity is more or less assured. When it comes to looking after your own interests, you are second to none. This is particularly true in the financial sphere and with regard to work.

30 SATURDAY *Moon Age Day 11 Moon Sign Scorpio*

am ....

pm..

Offers of travel may not seem quite as appealing as they could have done a few days ago and you might even be happy to stay in one place, as long as the company is stimulating. Love and romance is certainly to the forefront of many Capricorn minds today. All involvements with family members should be a joy at present.

1 SUNDAY *Moon Age Day 12 Moon Sign Sagittarius*

am ....

pm..

Your personal behaviour at the moment tends to be influenced by other-worldly intuition, maybe to such an extent that you can virtually hear what people are thinking. This side of your nature doesn't show very often, or usually anywhere near as strongly as it is right now.

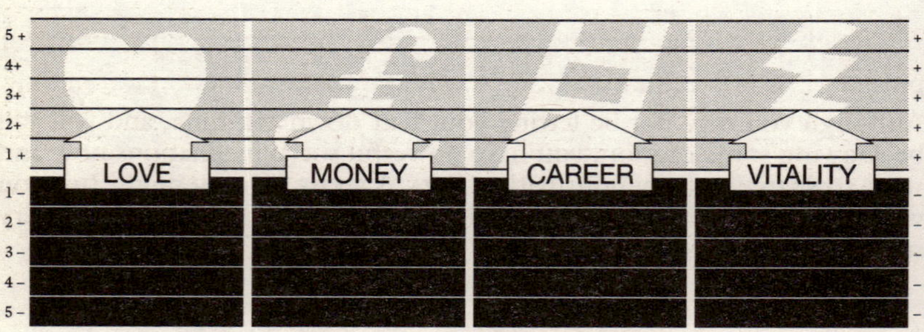

July 2012

YOUR MONTH AT A GLANCE

⊕ = Opportunities are around ● = Be on the defensive ● = Life is pretty ordinary

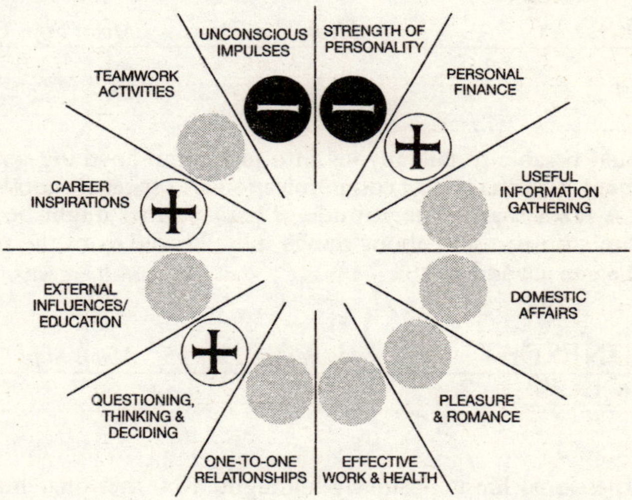

JULY HIGHS AND LOWS

Here I show you how the rhythms of the Moon will affect you this month. Like the tide, your energies and abilities will rise and fall with its pattern. When it is above the centre line, go for it, when it is below, you should be resting.

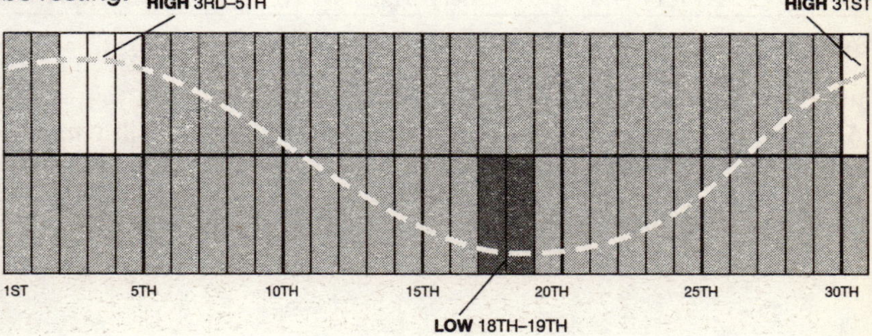

2 MONDAY *Moon Age Day 13 Moon Sign Sagittarius*

am ....

pm...

Domestic comfort really appeals at the moment and it looks as though the more progressive qualities of Capricorn are taking a holiday. This would be a wonderful period for relaxing at home, though you might find there is a wealth of things to get done before this proves to be possible.

3 TUESDAY *Moon Age Day 14 Moon Sign Capricorn*

am ....

pm...

You should be able to talk anyone into just about anything you wish at the moment. Your powers of communication are especially good and your intellect is razor sharp. The attitude of your partner might be puzzling unless you stop to think about things fully. People from the past enter your life again around now.

4 WEDNESDAY *Moon Age Day 15 Moon Sign Capricorn*

am ....

pm...

Your professional life is positively highlighted by the lunar high today. Even if you are not employed in a day-to-day sense, it is possible to make some extra money in one way or another. Finances are certainly on your mind and you could discover that you are better off than you previously thought.

5 THURSDAY *Moon Age Day 16 Moon Sign Capricorn*

am ....

pm...

At work, people are relying on you and it is certain you will come up with the goods when it proves important to do so. The attitude of some friends could be puzzling. High spirits and a positive attitude should be prevailing today, making this an excellent time to try out new skills.

6 FRIDAY *Moon Age Day 17 Moon Sign Aquarius*

am ....

pm ....

Life is generally rewarding and just as interesting as has been the case for the last week or so. The attitude of one or two friends might be puzzling but it also intrigues you and makes you want to investigate further. You should find that talks or simple encounters today can be very stimulating.

7 SATURDAY *Moon Age Day 18 Moon Sign Aquarius*

am ....

pm ....

Keep your eyes firmly fixed on the future and try to realise that feeling slightly below par today doesn't imply that this trend is likely to last. You are very responsive to the Moon at present and its influences never last long, whether they are positive or slightly negative. Your partner should be supportive.

8 SUNDAY *Moon Age Day 19 Moon Sign Pisces*

am ....

pm ....

Someone you haven't seen for quite some time could make a return to your life. Thoughts of travel could also be occupying your mind, perhaps making it difficult to concentrate on the more mundane aspects of life. You could find that much of today passes at a rapid pace.

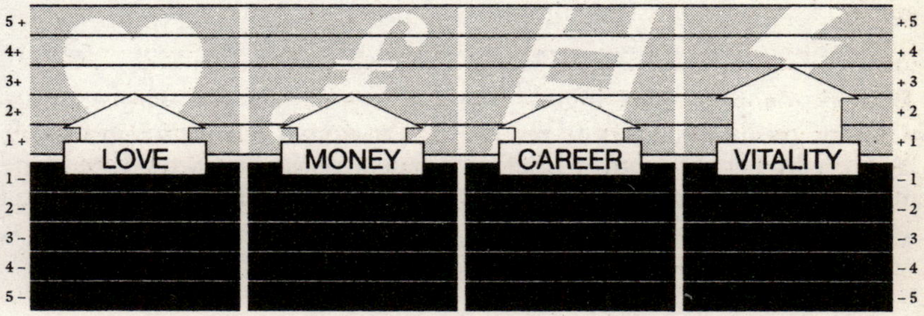

9 MONDAY *Moon Age Day 20 Moon Sign Pisces*

am...

pm...

Allying personal matters to your job, you find it quite easy to turn heads and should be the centre of attention most of the time. Stay away from pointless arguments and concentrate on having a good time when possible. You can be the main attraction in social groups at this stage of the working week.

10 TUESDAY *Moon Age Day 21 Moon Sign Aries*

am...

pm...

Facing problems, even small ones, head-on, is something you occasionally try to avoid doing but in the end you will have little choice. Someone you know well can be of tremendous help. Certain emotional issues rise to the surface at the moment, bringing you to a realisation that you need to address them.

11 WEDNESDAY *Moon Age Day 22 Moon Sign Aries*

am...

pm...

Conforming to expectations in a personal sense could provide the odd problem, so think carefully. Your judgement is now especially good and represents your single best quality for the moment. Not all attitudes that come your way are of equal merit and you need to be able to sort out the wheat from the chaff.

12 THURSDAY *Moon Age Day 23 Moon Sign Taurus*

am...

pm...

Use any means necessary to remove doubt from a relative's mind today. You could benefit from a brief withdrawal phase and would be quite happy doing something that simply suits you. Of course, there are still responsibilities to be dealt with, so you will probably want to get these out of the way as early in the day as you can manage.

13 FRIDAY *Moon Age Day 24 Moon Sign Taurus*

am ....

pm ....

Your ability to attract the right sort of people is noteworthy at this time. Concentrating on the matter at hand could be difficult early in the day because your mind is all over the place. If anything is going to take the edge off an otherwise perfect time, it is this slight and temporary inability to concentrate.

14 SATURDAY *Moon Age Day 25 Moon Sign Taurus*

am ....

pm ....

Confidence is generally high now and feeds you with a new type of inspiration. Someone who is going to be very important to your future makes an appearance in your life around now, so keep your eyes open. Your energy is quite noteworthy and represents your best chance of getting ahead at present.

15 SUNDAY ☿ *Moon Age Day 26 Moon Sign Gemini*

am ....

pm ....

Creature comforts seem important today and there is little doubt that Capricorn will enjoy the day best if it involves luxury and pleasure. See if you can organise a relaxing treat to make the best use of the influences. Try to remove as many unwanted obstacles from your life as you are able.

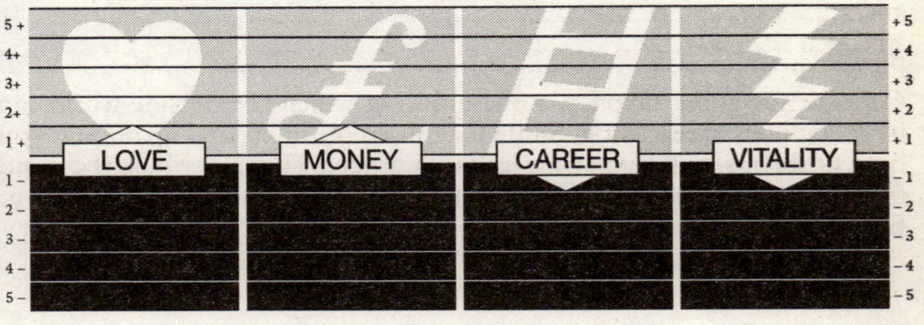

16 MONDAY ☿ *Moon Age Day 27 Moon Sign Gemini*

am ....

pm ....

This is a time when you should be involved with both social and group activities as they will put a smile on your face. Although Capricorn is very good when it comes to going it alone, this is not the way things are likely to be right now. The way friends are behaving is sure to stimulate your own sense of fun around this part of the week.

17 TUESDAY ☿ *Moon Age Day 28 Moon Sign Gemini*

am ....

pm ....

Although those you know well, both at home and at work, will be doing their best to lend a hand, what you require could well be beyond their abilities. It is probably slightly unwise to rely too heavily on others today. The answer is to do certain things for yourself. That way you can be certain they are done properly.

18 WEDNESDAY ☿ *Moon Age Day 29 Moon Sign Cancer*

am ....

pm ....

With the lunar low around it is difficult to genuinely take stock of present situations. Better by far to find something to distract you, though this is hardly likely to be anything adventurous or demanding. Everyone needs to recharge their batteries now and again and you are no exception.

19 THURSDAY ☿ *Moon Age Day 0 Moon Sign Cancer*

am ....

pm ....

Capricorn is going through a phase during which the outside world can look distinctly threatening. Settle for the simple in life and if you find you have problems, talk them through with others. There is still help around if you are willing to accept it. Your home is clearly the place you want to be most at the moment.

20 FRIDAY ☿ *Moon Age Day 1 Moon Sign Leo*

am ....

pm ....

Emotional upsets now tend to be very fleeting and so it isn't worth hanging on to them for any length of time. Instead, get on with something concrete and you will soon feel happier. Upsets in private relationships can distract you in ways far beyond the confines of your own front door, but only if you take them to heart.

21 SATURDAY ☿ *Moon Age Day 2 Moon Sign Leo*

am ....

pm ....

Too much financial speculation might be a mistake over the next few days. It's a good idea right now to check all facts very carefully and to be willing to listen to what those in the know are saying. Although this might mean taking the advice of someone you generally consider to be a rival, you can only gain as a result.

22 SUNDAY ☿ *Moon Age Day 3 Moon Sign Virgo*

am ....

pm ....

This is a good day for love, with declarations of affection coming from some unlikely or unexpected places and little confusion regarding your own feelings. There are certain financial matters that now deserve your attention. Some of your plans could be coming to fruition far earlier than you might have expected.

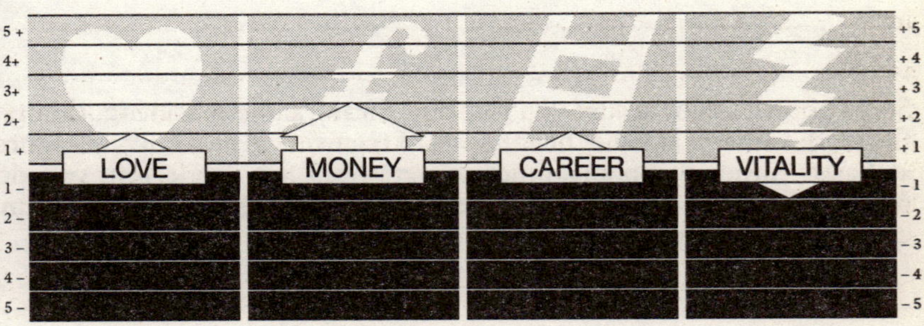

23 MONDAY ☿ *Moon Age Day 4 Moon Sign Virgo*

am ....

pm ....

If you have been considering throwing in your lot with any sort of group, go ahead. It seems you are in a more 'give and take' frame of mind than might sometimes be the case. This could lead to an interesting sort of day and one during which co-operation pays dividends for everyone concerned.

24 TUESDAY ☿ *Moon Age Day 5 Moon Sign Libra*

am ....

pm ....

Your powers of attraction are in the ascendant and so you should not be in the least surprised to find that attention is coming from all manner of directions. In a personal sense this might provide a very slightly embarrassing situation and one that means having to politely tell someone if you are spoken for romantically.

25 WEDNESDAY ☿ *Moon Age Day 6 Moon Sign Libra*

am ....

pm ....

You might now discover a more sporting side to your nature and one that you can exploit fully. This is not a good time to treat everything you hear as fact, even if to do so makes for a more comfortable ride. Check and check again, this is the key to greater progress in the medium-term.

26 THURSDAY ☿ *Moon Age Day 7 Moon Sign Libra*

am ....

pm ....

Some people might accuse you of being sneaky and self-seeking, though the truth is that you have the interests of relatives, friends and colleagues at heart. Although opportunities to get ahead are not legion, you do recognise them well and will make the effort to squeeze through any crack to get what you want.

27 FRIDAY ☿ *Moon Age Day 8 Moon Sign Scorpio*

am..

pm..

Some compensation for a past problem might be forthcoming soon. You are probably motivated today by the need to get colleagues working along the same lines you are choosing for yourself. Try hard to persuade, rather than to bully, because the way things appear is everything at the moment.

28 SATURDAY ☿ *Moon Age Day 9 Moon Sign Scorpio*

am..

pm..

You now need to be certain of your facts, as is always the case for Capricorn. Do a little research. When you have, decide what is the best course of action and follow it. A slight lack of confidence in your own ideas or abilities might get in the way of advancement at the moment.

29 SUNDAY ☿ *Moon Age Day 10 Moon Sign Sagittarius*

am..

pm..

Routines are likely to bore you today, so avoid them. Along comes a socially helpful period, during which those around you are more willing than ever to put themselves out on your behalf. Don't be too quick to judge the actions or opinions of a friend, but stay open-minded, flexible and even suggestible.

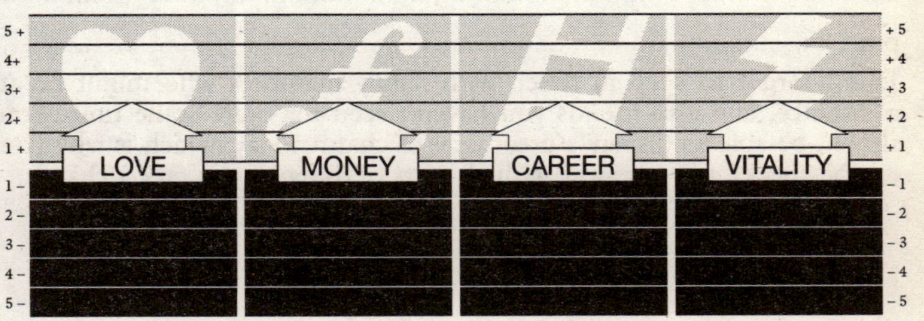

30 MONDAY ☿ *Moon Age Day 11 Moon Sign Sagittarius*

am ....

pm ....

A day off work would suit you well today. Just because you are somewhat withdrawn at the moment, doesn't indicate that you are failing to come up with some startling ideas – think things through in your mind. Getting away from the rat race appeals to you at this stage of the week.

31 TUESDAY ☿ *Moon Age Day 12 Moon Sign Capricorn*

am ....

pm ....

Decisions you take at the moment tend to be quite lucky, a situation for which you can thank the lunar high. It's time to go for gold and to trust in your own judgement, which tends to be very sound now. Travel is worth considering, with holidays beckoning, or trips planned at short notice.

1 WEDNESDAY ☿ *Moon Age Day 13 Moon Sign Capricorn*

am ....

pm ....

Things change quickly as the lunar high continues to take hold of your life. The timidity that could have been evident a few days ago now disappears altogether, leaving you feeling extra confident and anxious to make a big impression. That shouldn't be difficult, especially in a social sense.

2 THURSDAY ☿ *Moon Age Day 14 Moon Sign Aquarius*

am ....

pm ....

Don't forget to keep in touch with family members who might be at a distance, and also friends you haven't seen for quite some time. You should be able to display a great deal of charm today, which is why you can be cheeky and get away with all sorts of things if you take a chance.

3 FRIDAY ☿ *Moon Age Day 15 Moon Sign Aquarius*

am ....

pm ....

Confidence is definitely on the increase and is stimulated by the number of people calling upon you for advice. In a professional sense, you should be able to bring a situation to a satisfactory conclusion and should find that you have a strong 'edge' when dealing with those who have a different strategy.

4 SATURDAY ☿ *Moon Age Day 16 Moon Sign Pisces*

am ....

pm ....

A little extra care is necessary now. Getting ahead with specific plans today can bring a number of pitfalls, all of which you have to address very carefully. Although you have a good ability to concentrate, it is true that demands are being made of you. By the evening, you could easily retreat into romance and all it offers.

5 SUNDAY ☿ *Moon Age Day 17 Moon Sign Pisces*

am ....

pm ....

Be certain of what you want from life and then decide how to get it. Since there are so many people around who want to help you out, there is little chance of failure. Your ego is boosted tremendously, at what can turn out to be one of the most progressive phases during the whole of August.

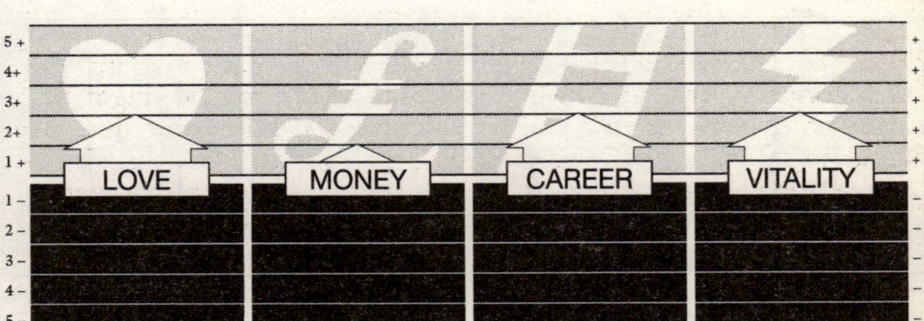

August

2012

Your Month at a Glance

(+) = Opportunities are around (−) = Be on the defensive (●) = Life is pretty ordinary

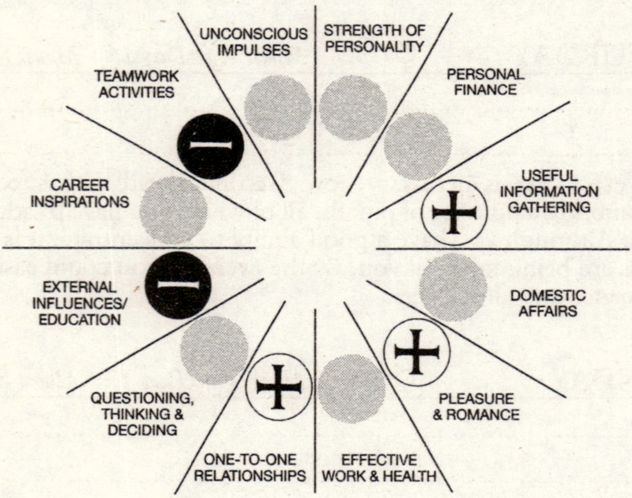

August Highs and Lows

Here I show you how the rhythms of the Moon will affect you this month. Like the tide, your energies and abilities will rise and fall with its pattern. When it is above the centre line, go for it, when it is below, you should be resting.

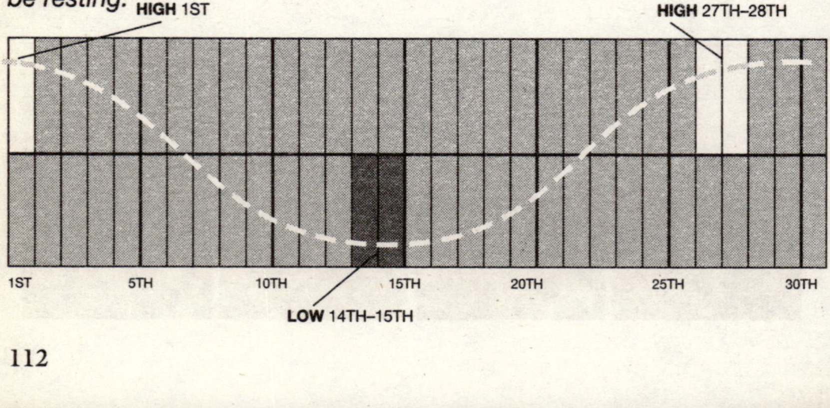

6 MONDAY ☿ *Moon Age Day 18 Moon Sign Aries*

am ....

pm ....

Chill out when someone is trying to annoy you, because you won't gain any house points by rising to the bait. It might be best not to get involved in heated discussions of any sort. A beneficial high-energy period is maintained, as you zip through chores in a quarter of the time they would usually take.

7 TUESDAY ☿ *Moon Age Day 19 Moon Sign Aries*

am ....

pm ....

Trying to get a Capricorn to do anything that goes against the grain is more or less impossible. Your stubborn streak is showing strongly now. With regard to getting everyday matters sorted today, your attitude might be at fault. There are some tasks you simply don't want to undertake, it's as simple as that.

8 WEDNESDAY ☿ *Moon Age Day 20 Moon Sign Aries*

am ....

pm ....

It might not be very easy to see your way forward, particularly in a financial sense, but there are always people around who will offer sound advice and a helping hand. Close emotional attachments work better for you today than casual friendships or even associations at work.

9 THURSDAY *Moon Age Day 21 Moon Sign Taurus*

am ....

pm ....

Give and take are important factors in relationships, and particularly those with a romantic content. Be prepared to be singled out around now, this time entirely favourably. There are influences increasing your ego energy and making it possible for you to redress the slightly less than favourable balance of yesterday.

10 FRIDAY *Moon Age Day 22 Moon Sign Taurus*

am ....

pm ....

The fact is that you are feeling a little lack-lustre today and will be happier to let someone else take the strain. Some great chances are not too far away and it is likely that you will actively want to plan ahead of them. That requires time to think. You may decide to wind down certain activities, at least for the moment.

11 SATURDAY *Moon Age Day 23 Moon Sign Gemini*

am ....

pm ....

Popularity is likely, and the smell of greater success is in your nostrils. Slowly but surely, the fact that both the Sun and Mars are so well aspected for you is increasing the odds of you getting more of what you really want from life. You should find you have plenty of energy and enthusiasm for whatever you choose to do.

12 SUNDAY *Moon Age Day 24 Moon Sign Gemini*

am ....

pm ....

Sort out any minor irritations in the family early on and then you will be free to do whatever takes your fancy. Some Capricorns see this as being a time for turning over a new leaf. Domestic matters can get in the way of your personal freedoms, something you don't want to happen during today.

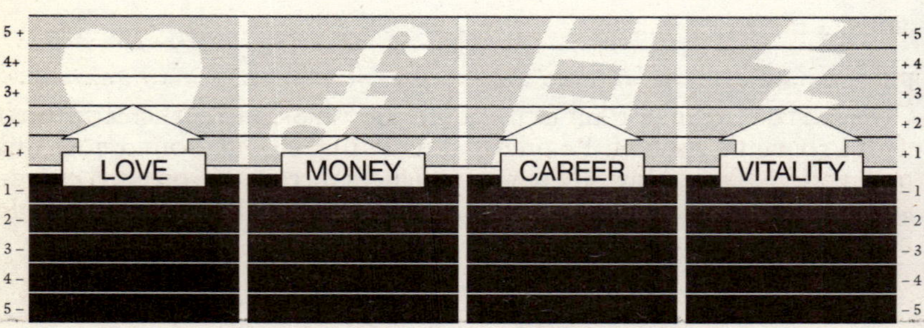

13 MONDAY *Moon Age Day 25 Moon Sign Gemini*

am ....

pm ....

Concentrate on the task at hand when at work and then remain determined to have a good time later. Schedules and deadlines might be a little frustrating, though you'll resolve that. It is clear that you intend to be noticed today and that isn't surprising because in one way and another you are putting on a very good show.

14 TUESDAY *Moon Age Day 26 Moon Sign Cancer*

am ....

pm ....

Your personal influence is somewhat restricted by the lunar low, though this time around it tends to be with regard to practical matters. For this reason you should spend at least part of today doing what pleases you, even though these things don't have a great deal of bearing on your overall future.

15 WEDNESDAY *Moon Age Day 27 Moon Sign Cancer*

am ....

pm ....

Keeping expectations moderate is what matters now. Confidence is low during the two days that the Moon is in your opposite sign, and pushing against the tide is unlikely to work. Stay chatty and confident, planning carefully and looking towards greater movement later in the week.

16 THURSDAY *Moon Age Day 28 Moon Sign Leo*

am ....

pm ....

What matters most about today are the hours when you are not at work. Not only do things look particularly good on the romantic front, but you will also find yourself making a favourable impression on strangers. You may have to focus on minor tasks today because it's the little jobs that add up to successes later on.

17 FRIDAY *Moon Age Day 0 Moon Sign Leo*

am..

pm..

A joint financial venture could prove to be something of a headache and you need to be careful that you have thought everything through carefully. Meanwhile, there could be events happening in the family that both please and displease you for different reasons. Striking the right balance in your relationships takes tact.

18 SATURDAY *Moon Age Day 1 Moon Sign Leo*

am..

pm..

What you definitely don't need at this time of year is to be stuck indoors, with no view of nature and no gentle breeze blowing across your face. Try to get away somewhere around this time. Even if you don't have a holiday planned, a short change of scene would do you the world of good, if you can manage it.

19 SUNDAY *Moon Age Day 2 Moon Sign Virgo*

am..

pm..

Expect social offers to come in at the last minute and that you will find it difficult to refuse them. Particularly if you are working, today's trends show that you are pushing onward and upward in matters associated with career. If, on the other hand, you have the next couple of days to yourself, you might choose a degree of excitement.

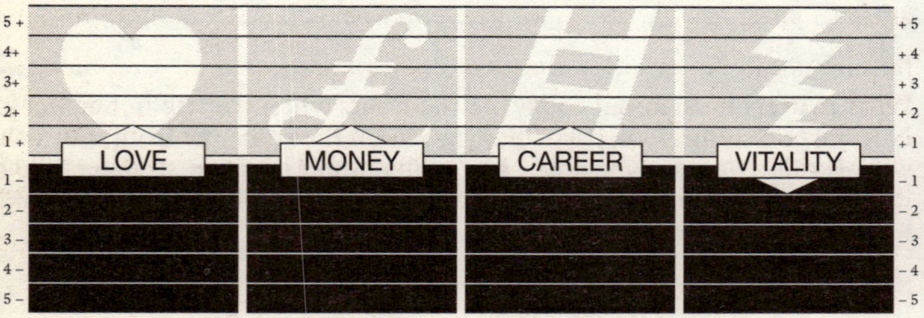

20 MONDAY *Moon Age Day 3 Moon Sign Virgo*

am ....

pm..

Confidence isn't hard to engender in almost any situation and you should be looking particularly good in social settings and when faced with romantic proposals. With plenty of incentive, a supercharged ego begins to emerge. Although it isn't your way to sing your own praises, you could be doing so now.

21 TUESDAY *Moon Age Day 4 Moon Sign Libra*

am ....

pm..

You should have the confidence to say what you think and the slightly dark aspect of some recent days ought to have disappeared altogether. There ought to be time now to get things done at home that you know will make you more comfortable later. This could be a high-spirited and deeply romantic time.

22 WEDNESDAY *Moon Age Day 5 Moon Sign Libra*

am ....

pm..

Compliments could be coming your way from unlikely directions. Try not to let domestic responsibilities get in the way of things you would rather be doing. It pays dividends to think in advance and to make sure all those chores are out of the way so that you can concentrate on having fun.

23 THURSDAY *Moon Age Day 6 Moon Sign Scorpio*

am ....

pm..

Allow things to happen in their own good time. If you are constantly reacting, it is possible that you are not using either your intuition or your common sense enough. There are many changes around just now and you'll be trying hard to keep life on an even keel. Actually, it could be the case that you are trying too hard.

24 FRIDAY *Moon Age Day 7 Moon Sign Scorpio*

am ....

pm ....

Keep on looking for those wide, open spaces. This is a holiday time generally but turns out to be an especially good time for you to take a break. If you cannot get away from the rat race, at least leave some time free at some stage during the day. Even a walk in the park would be better than nothing.

25 SATURDAY *Moon Age Day 8 Moon Sign Sagittarius*

am ....

pm ....

In romantic attachments, you can demonstrate that you are faithful and quite willing to take the rough with the smooth. The weekend finds you looking for adventure and fun. Unfortunately some trends are not at their best and you might have to make do with smaller trips or perhaps a shopping spree.

26 SUNDAY *Moon Age Day 9 Moon Sign Sagittarius*

am ....

pm ....

You should find yourself well able to keep up with the few demands that are being made of you but there ought to be enough time you can call your own. A mixture of activity and relaxation is what works best for you at the moment. Benefits come mainly from friends this Sunday.

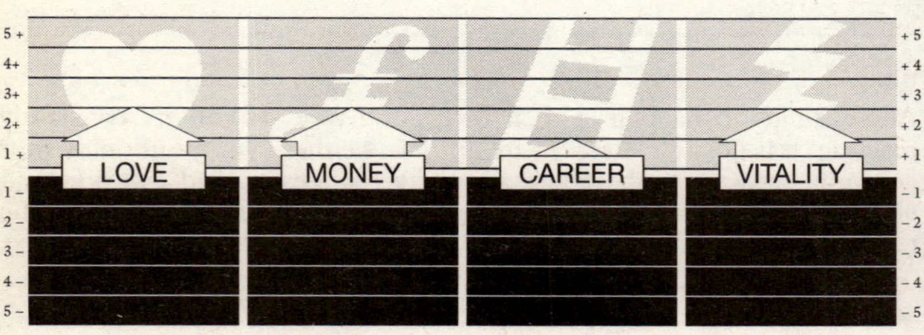

27 MONDAY *Moon Age Day 10 Moon Sign Capricorn*

am ....

pm ....

You can get a great deal today, just from showing some cheek. This isn't normally your way but the trends are generally very good and there is little to prevent you from making significant headway. Get an early start with all major plans and don't hold back when it comes to telling people what you think.

28 TUESDAY *Moon Age Day 11 Moon Sign Capricorn*

am ....

pm ....

Your influence is extremely strong at this time and it isn't just because of the lunar high. You have been gradually increasing your persuasive ways to such an extent that you will be able to get even the most awkward types on side. This is a day during which you will find it possible to talk anyone into doing anything you wish.

29 WEDNESDAY *Moon Age Day 12 Moon Sign Aquarius*

am ....

pm ....

Attention to matters of health might seem important but avoid worrying too much about situations that are not at all what they seem. Right now the key to success seems to lie with your career. You will also need to deal with a few nagging details, even though these can prove to be quite tedious at times.

30 THURSDAY *Moon Age Day 13 Moon Sign Aquarius*

am ....

pm ....

It looks as though an exchange of ideas and views could turn out to be very useful right now and there are plenty of people around who you could call on. In the end, probably the most unlikely individual is your chosen resort, though you should definitely stay away from people who have difficulty in keeping their own secrets, let alone yours.

31 FRIDAY *Moon Age Day 14 Moon Sign Pisces*

am ....

pm ....

Acting on impulse, something you rarely do, is a way to create a truly exciting day. Personalities come into your life around this time and might bring new attitudes and modes of behaviour that you wish to adopt. You have a bright, quick mind and remain determined to force situations to work out the way you would wish.

1 SATURDAY *Moon Age Day 15 Moon Sign Pisces*

am ....

pm ....

You could so easily find yourself in a prominent position today, so you will need to keep your wits about you. Being in the limelight is a double-edged sword for Capricorn – you often like it but sometimes hate it as well. Fortunately, you are not feeling particularly shy at present.

2 SUNDAY *Moon Age Day 16 Moon Sign Pisces*

am ....

pm ....

Today is comprised, in part, of positive social encounters, most of which are geared towards improving your personal situation. Your mind is sharp and your sense of humour definitely intact. This gives you the ability to get ahead of the game and to show the world at large what you are made of.

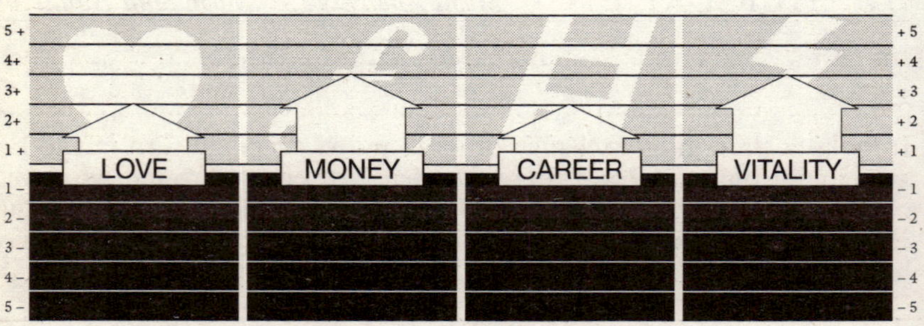

September

2012

Your Month at a Glance

⊕ = Opportunities are around ⊖ = Be on the defensive ● = Life is pretty ordinary

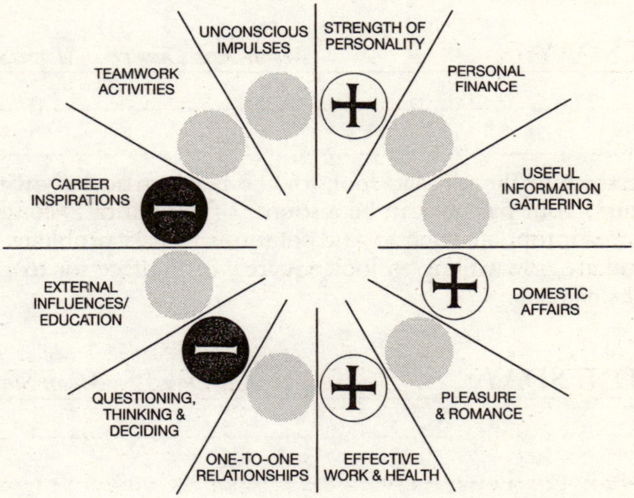

September Highs and Lows

Here I show you how the rhythms of the Moon will affect you this month. Like the tide, your energies and abilities will rise and fall with its pattern. When it is above the centre line, go for it, when it is below, you should be resting.

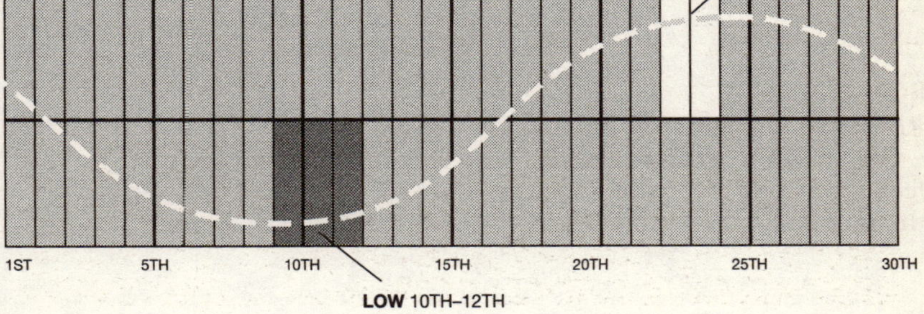

3 MONDAY *Moon Age Day 17 Moon Sign Aries*

am ....

pm ....

Decide what you want from life and then go for it, even though you might be somewhat nervous about the potential consequences. At the same time, it would be good to pace yourself, because arriving at any winning post too far ahead of the competition gets you noticed in ways you don't really want.

4 TUESDAY *Moon Age Day 18 Moon Sign Aries*

am ....

pm ....

It's time to shun the old and look for the new, particularly within your own nature. Your partner can be a source of inspiration. Along comes a more than appropriate time to find solutions to past problems, some of which you are now willing to look squarely in the face for the first time in months or years.

5 WEDNESDAY *Moon Age Day 19 Moon Sign Taurus*

am ....

pm ....

Almost anything can prove to be a stimulus to your investigative skills, but especially situations that are genuinely odd or curious. Not everyone will share your fascination, and you may have to explain yourself, probably with humour. There is more than one planetary aspect around now that can make you extremely inquisitive.

6 THURSDAY *Moon Age Day 20 Moon Sign Taurus*

am ....

pm ....

Romantic attachments have rarely looked better, and you should be willing to go to great lengths to tell a romantic partner the way you really feel about them. Personal matters, though carrying a few challenges at the moment, can be concluded to your satisfaction in the end.

7 FRIDAY *Moon Age Day 21 Moon Sign Taurus*

am ....

pm..

It appears that information you receive, probably via a friend, will show conclusively how much others think about your organisational skills and general competence. This ought to make you feel much better about yourself and recent efforts you have made. If it doesn't, then you are not being honest.

8 SATURDAY *Moon Age Day 22 Moon Sign Gemini*

am ....

pm..

As long as you are being genuinely true to yourself, all is well now. What won't work at the moment is trying to fool someone, even though you are simply trying to avoid hurting them. Emotional matters can put you in the hot seat, though probably not if you make sure you explain yourself right from the start.

9 SUNDAY *Moon Age Day 23 Moon Sign Gemini*

am ....

pm..

It should not be hard to broaden your horizons or to see the wider picture in just about any situation today. What won't please you too much would be a whole raft of rules and regulations, most of which seem custom-made to throw you. In the end, answers that come your way should be highly satisfying.

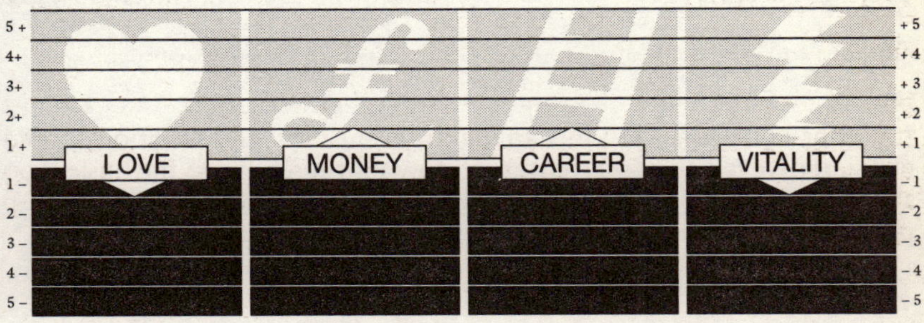

10 MONDAY *Moon Age Day 24 Moon Sign Cancer*

am ....

pm ....

It's time to slow things down somewhat and to accept the steadier pace demanded by the Moon in Cancer. Thoughtful and even deeply contemplative, this ought to be the sort of day when you engage in steady hobbies or interests. In the main, you should stay away from contentious or difficult issues.

11 TUESDAY *Moon Age Day 25 Moon Sign Cancer*

am ....

pm ....

Although you fail to make any real headway at work right now, you can enjoy what personal relationships throw in your path. The attitude of friends can be quite puzzling at present. You remain in the middle of a lull and there isn't really much you can do to counter the situation, so you may as well enjoy it.

12 WEDNESDAY *Moon Age Day 26 Moon Sign Cancer*

am ....

pm ....

There should be plenty of compliments coming your way, leading to some confusion in your mind regarding the way others think about you. Try to use the better potential coming your way with regard to money to handle cash well. Looking ahead isn't difficult, so use your shrewd but speculative frame of mind.

13 THURSDAY *Moon Age Day 27 Moon Sign Leo*

am ....

pm ....

If you have been lacking in stamina in recent days, the situation should now improve. Challenges are something you will relish and the busier you are, the better you are likely to feel. You should now be feeling buoyed up physically and ready to face whatever challenges come your way.

14 FRIDAY *Moon Age Day 28 Moon Sign Leo*

am ....

pm ....

You should be quite satisfied with the state of play in personal attachments and also show a chance of gaining significantly when it comes to acquiring both possessions and money. Although you have plenty to do today, there are still potential gains to be made away from the mainstream of practical living.

15 SATURDAY *Moon Age Day 29 Moon Sign Virgo*

am ....

pm ....

Try not to be too fussy about details and stick to what you know when it comes to public discussions. This is a time of steady but relentless building, both in a financial and a personal sense. As a result, you should be quite happy because the most positive associations of Capricorn are given endless scope, especially your common sense.

16 SUNDAY *Moon Age Day 0 Moon Sign Virgo*

am ....

pm ....

You need to be in the company of interesting people if you want to get the most out of the day and should be thinking in terms of individuals who have an exciting attitude to life. Mundane matters could prove to be somewhat tiresome today and you will want to ring the changes just as much as you can.

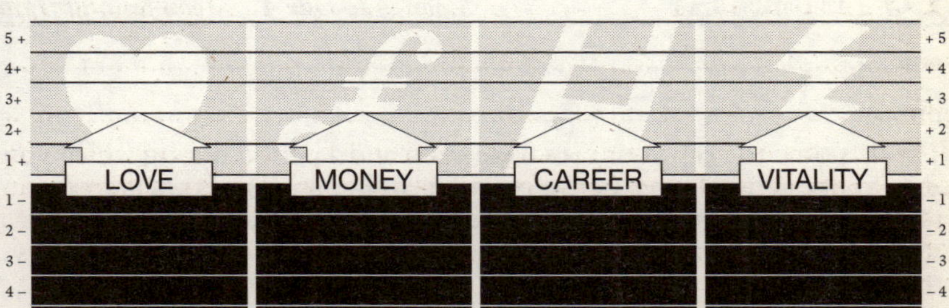

17 MONDAY *Moon Age Day 1 Moon Sign Libra*

am ....

pm ....

Concentrate on specific jobs at work and don't be put off by those with a negative attitude. Your ego is on the increase and this might lead to one or two other people looking at you sideways. So often, you go through life without making a ripple on the water, so when you are up-front it can come as a surprise.

18 TUESDAY *Moon Age Day 2 Moon Sign Libra*

am ....

pm ....

Avoid family rows and if possible do what you can to prevent them. A change of scene for today would probably do everyone a lot of good. You seem to be rather pushy today, probably because you are anxious to get ahead and to use almost any means at your disposal to prove your capabilities.

19 WEDNESDAY *Moon Age Day 3 Moon Sign Scorpio*

am ....

pm ....

There is a slight tendency for you to retreat into yourself today, something that perhaps should be avoided around now. Money matters seem to strengthen but this is probably more a state of mind. Try to vary your routines as much as you can today because tedium follows if you always do the expected thing.

20 THURSDAY *Moon Age Day 4 Moon Sign Scorpio*

am ....

pm ....

This is a time to keep your eyes wide open and a period during which you should not allow the restrictive practices and opinions of others to get in the way. Avoid family arguments. There are both major and minor gains staring you in the face today, the question is whether or not you realise this fact.

21 FRIDAY *Moon Age Day 5 Moon Sign Sagittarius*

am ....

pm ....

Although you seem to have somewhat less influence over others today, they are in reality taking a great deal of notice of your opinions. You can expect a quiet couple of days, whilst the Moon passes through your solar twelfth house. This is probably just as well with a period of intense activity in view.

22 SATURDAY *Moon Age Day 6 Moon Sign Sagittarius*

am ....

pm ....

You should have a quiet start to the weekend but this is not a situation that is going to last very long. Routines seem to be rewarding at first but could become tedious later so get them dealt with early on. A period of social harmony now comes along, so arrange to get together with friends.

23 SUNDAY *Moon Age Day 7 Moon Sign Capricorn*

am ....

pm ....

It's hard to keep a sense of proportion now and there is some doubt as to whether you should. Let your mind work on potential problems because your ability to get to grips with life is incredible. The lunar high changes everything today because out of a fairly introspective phase, you are catapulted into activity.

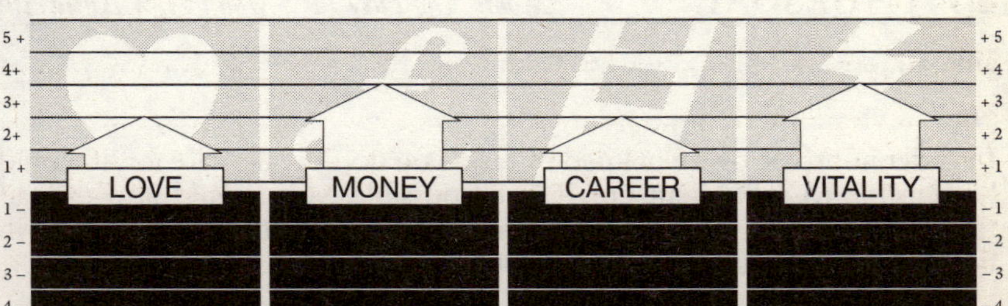

24 MONDAY *Moon Age Day 8 Moon Sign Capricorn*

am ....

pm ....

Someone you haven't seen for a while could come back to your life now and bring with them a host of new possibilities. This may be the best day of the month in an overall sense. Things should still be going well for you and this is the time of the month when Lady Luck is definitely on your side.

25 TUESDAY *Moon Age Day 9 Moon Sign Aquarius*

am ....

pm ....

Although in a mental sense you are now sharper than ever, you can still confuse yourself if you try hard enough. The fact is that you are likely to find the right answer to most problems immediately but you don't realise the fact and go on worrying about matters longer than is either necessary or wise.

26 WEDNESDAY *Moon Age Day 10 Moon Sign Aquarius*

am ....

pm ....

It could so easily seem as though you are not being particularly efficient right now. The truth is that you are very self-critical and inclined to expect more of yourself than is reasonable. If you don't believe you are making adequate progress, ask someone else. They will do all they can to convince you.

27 THURSDAY *Moon Age Day 11 Moon Sign Aquarius*

am ....

pm ....

In order not to be overwhelmed by tasks you don't really care for, it would be sensible to split them up. If at all possible, you should also offload them on to those who are willing to lend a hand. Positive highlights in both social and romantic matters could be the order of the day now.

28 FRIDAY *Moon Age Day 12 Moon Sign Pisces*

am..

pm..

You seem to be in the right frame of mind to get things done in a very social way. That obviously means co-operation, something you excel at right now. When you need to be forceful you can pull out the stops but don't overdo it. Decisions are important now but there is plenty of help making them.

29 SATURDAY *Moon Age Day 13 Moon Sign Pisces*

am..

pm..

Slow and steady wins the race for you this weekend and you need to look at potential problems one at a time, rather than allowing them to wash over you in waves. You might be in too much of a rush early in the day – if this turns out to be the case, expect to make a few mistakes.

30 SUNDAY *Moon Age Day 14 Moon Sign Aries*

am..

pm..

Your sense of adventure is back in great measure and you wouldn't take kindly to being held back. You may even be rather more competitive than usual so if there is some sort of competition around, you may want to enter it. Capricorns who have been a little out sorts of late should find that they are feeling better now.

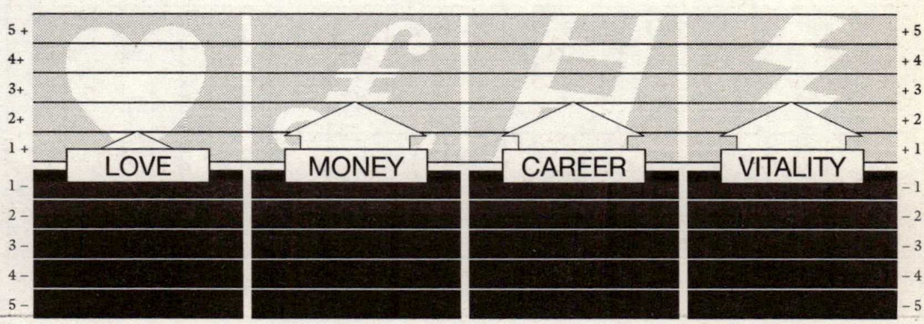

October

2012

Your Month at a Glance

(+) = Opportunities are around (–) = Be on the defensive (●) = Life is pretty ordinary

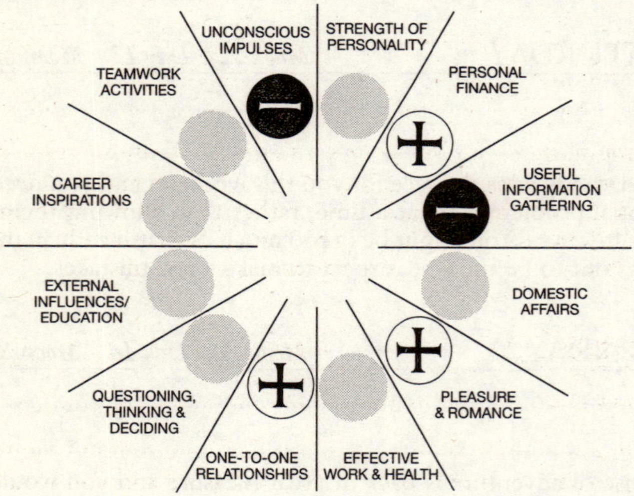

October Highs and Lows

Here I show you how the rhythms of the Moon will affect you this month. Like the tide, your energies and abilities will rise and fall with its pattern. When it is above the centre line, go for it, when it is below, you should be resting.

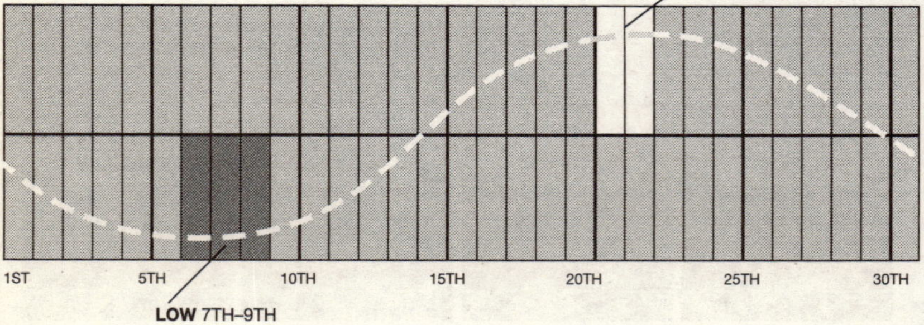

1 MONDAY *Moon Age Day 15 Moon Sign Aries*

am ....

pm ....

Keep your eyes open and make a definite decision if offers are already on the table. This is a day when you are once again casting your mind forward, and particularly so in a work sense. It could be that new responsibilities are on offer, or maybe you simply want to ring the changes altogether.

2 TUESDAY *Moon Age Day 16 Moon Sign Taurus*

am ....

pm ....

Give some extra attention to your personal life, and start by telling your partner how important they are to you. Be prepared to enjoy what should be an active and very enterprising day but don't take your eye off the ball in terms of work. Romance is likely to play a significant role in your life today.

3 WEDNESDAY *Moon Age Day 17 Moon Sign Taurus*

am ....

pm ....

Perhaps somewhat uncharacteristically you are very demonstrative now. This is not the most comfortable situation for a Capricorn subject and you may find a little embarrassment involved in some of your contacts with others. However, there's no reason at all to feel shy about telling someone how much you care.

4 THURSDAY *Moon Age Day 18 Moon Sign Taurus*

am ....

pm ....

Capricorn is now playing in the major league as far as romance is concerned. There are likely to be people coming into your life around now who you haven't met before. This turns out to be a very fortunate time for new contacts, some of whom could turn out to be valued and trusted friends in the longer term.

5 FRIDAY *Moon Age Day 19 Moon Sign Gemini*

am ....

pm..

It's true that you are not exactly lucky at the moment but most Capricorns realise that with hard work and application they make their own luck. How true this is for you right now. If it is better financial circumstances you have been looking for, then this could turn out to be very much your most favourable period.

6 SATURDAY *Moon Age Day 20 Moon Sign Gemini*

am ....

pm..

There are planetary aspects around now that show how much you have to offer to social groups and to your family. Friends should prove to be especially helpful at the moment and might have some news that could brighten your day no end. Energy and determination won't be in short supply when you need them the most.

7 SUNDAY *Moon Age Day 21 Moon Sign Cancer*

am ....

pm..

There are a few setbacks today, mostly brought about by the presence of the lunar low. This means they are more in your mind than in reality but it amounts to the same thing in the end. Stay interested in something and don't spend the whole day doing things that reflect the worse aspects of your state of mind.

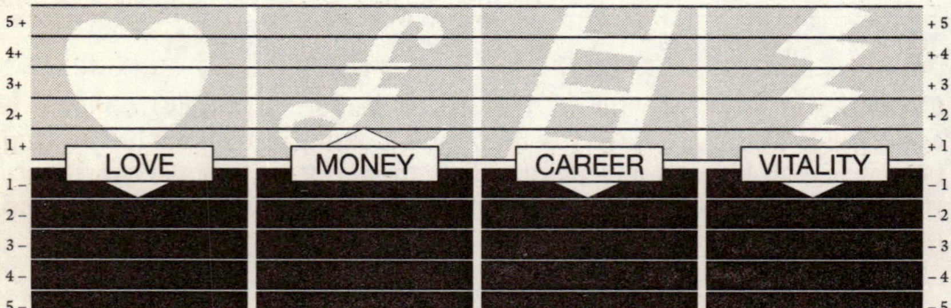

8 MONDAY *Moon Age Day 22 Moon Sign Cancer*

am ....

pm ....

Fairly inevitably, the pace is slower today and you will have to accept this fact. It isn't that the lunar low is likely to depress you, or cause any undue problem. Rather you are likely to discover that continued progress now slows down so much that you realise the best way to deal with circumstances is to wait a while.

9 TUESDAY *Moon Age Day 23 Moon Sign Cancer*

am ....

pm ....

There's no doubt about it. You have it within you to bring out the best in others today, as long as you put yourself out to do so. You can bring joy into other people's lives. Plus, on a more selfish footing, once you have them on your side it is possible for you to gain as a result. There's no sin in getting what you want occasionally.

10 WEDNESDAY *Moon Age Day 24 Moon Sign Leo*

am ....

pm ....

Deal quickly with everyday matters that are important to you, even though you may not have the inclination. Maybe just a little more drive and enthusiasm would turn out to be useful. In general though, the pace of life is neither too fast nor too slow, which is just the way you love things to be.

11 THURSDAY *Moon Age Day 25 Moon Sign Leo*

am ....

pm ....

Keep discussions with others away from the everyday subjects of life and allow your mind to wander into the realms of the possible. You don't always daydream quite as much as you should because the practical quality of your nature gets in the way. Now you can both talk and maybe write as a visionary.

12 FRIDAY *Moon Age Day 26 Moon Sign Virgo*

am ....

pm..

Not everyone is on the same wavelength as you are when it comes to new ideas but you do have the power to persuade them. Today you should be able to get away with almost anything. Certainly a little cheek goes a long way and you know how to make others laugh, which is half the battle won.

13 SATURDAY *Moon Age Day 27 Moon Sign Virgo*

am ....

pm..

Try not to have to work too hard today, maybe even taking a holiday if you are a weekend worker. Don't be surprised if this turns out to be a 'more of the same' sort of day. However, trends are gradually building up that mean you should soon be looking far ahead in terms of travel and ultimate enjoyment of life.

14 SUNDAY *Moon Age Day 28 Moon Sign Libra*

am ....

pm..

Don't be tardy about getting away from it all and accept almost any offer of a trip that comes along at the moment. There are people around you haven't seen for some time and now is as good a time as any to rekindle what was once a bright flame. The more adventure you can get into your life, the greater the rewards.

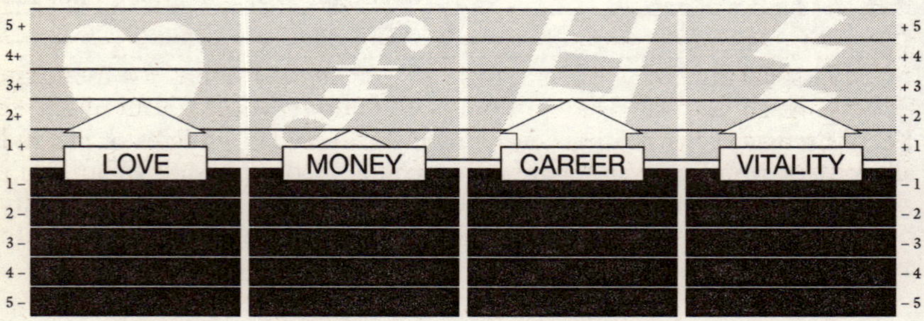

15 MONDAY *Moon Age Day 0 Moon Sign Libra*

am ....

pm..

It will be obvious that much of your energy is presently channelled into your work – no bad thing since you have so much of it. There is assistance to call upon if you find yourself out of your depth at any stage but there is also a good chance you will not accept the help that is around. Try not to be too proud for your own good.

16 TUESDAY *Moon Age Day 1 Moon Sign Libra*

am ....

pm..

Now friendships prove to be especially rewarding and it is clear that you would do almost anything for the pals who are so important to you. That's fine but you can't run their lives for them. Be on hand if necessary but in the final analysis stand back and allow people a degree of latitude.

17 WEDNESDAY *Moon Age Day 2 Moon Sign Scorpio*

am ....

pm..

Take note of the way the world is watching you and be sure to make the most of some very useful trends. Your mind is sharp and most of your intuitive insights are well worth following. One of the most important factors today is that others are giving you credit for having good ideas.

18 THURSDAY *Moon Age Day 3 Moon Sign Scorpio*

am ....

pm..

Socially speaking, your life is a buzz of activity and there are moments during which you will want to slow matters down a little. Your ability to get your message across is still extremely good. The domestic scene is a busy place, with people coming and going all the time.

19 FRIDAY *Moon Age Day 4 Moon Sign Sagittarius*

am ....

pm ....

Although as a general rule you are quite willing to do whatever you can for others, they will not always be particularly pleased to have you around. There are times when it is sensible to lend a hand and other occasions when it is much better to simply mind your own business. Some discretion is called for today.

20 SATURDAY *Moon Age Day 5 Moon Sign Sagittarius*

am ....

pm ....

This may not be the most exciting day you will register this month because you have to deal with a twelfth house Moon, but tomorrow will bring definite change. The more you can do to help others move forward in their own lives, the better you also manage to feel about what is happening to you.

21 SUNDAY *Moon Age Day 6 Moon Sign Capricorn*

am ....

pm ....

Pottering around in the house won't be at all what appeals to you the most right now, because it's clear you need to be getting out and about. Anything cultural is likely to appeal to you today and the physical needs of your Earth-sign body also have to be kept in mind at the moment, so a long walk might be in order.

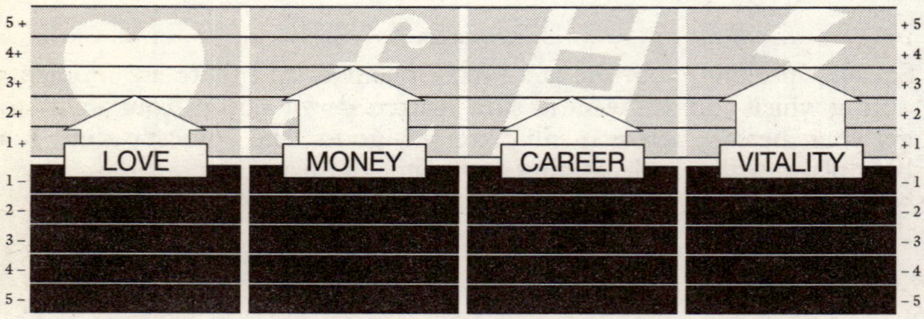

22 MONDAY *Moon Age Day 7 Moon Sign Capricorn*

am ....

pm ....

The green light is still on, bringing a very positive and influential start to the week. Although you are still motivated towards material success you should also find enough time simply to have fun. The bearing your attitude has on family members and particularly your partner is marked.

23 TUESDAY *Moon Age Day 8 Moon Sign Aquarius*

am ....

pm ....

Keep up your efforts to move ahead professionally and listen to the wise advice of some very good friends at this time. Right now, outdoor activities seem to have a particular reward. Maybe the sporting side of your nature is beginning to show or it could be that you just feel like a walk in the fresh air.

24 WEDNESDAY *Moon Age Day 9 Moon Sign Aquarius*

am ....

pm ....

Don't be too quick to judge the actions of your friends today. This is a time when you can get on well in a practical sense. Taking all you have learned in the past, you apply your experience to matters in the practical world and come up with answers that others will think have a hint of genius about them.

25 THURSDAY *Moon Age Day 10 Moon Sign Pisces*

am ....

pm ....

Avoid confusion in personal matters by explaining yourself. You want to have your own way and you decide that you are going to get it now. This is the less attractive face of Capricorn as far as other people are concerned and you should at least try to modify the slightly selfish qualities that show at this time.

26 FRIDAY *Moon Age Day 11 Moon Sign Pisces*

am ....

pm..

Capricorn is very practical and capable, a fact that shows all too clearly at this time. Your 'leave it to me' attitude will be popular with quite a few people today and it is true that you seem to be able to do things on your own that are more difficult in groups. You are less likely to go it alone in personal matters.

27 SATURDAY *Moon Age Day 12 Moon Sign Aries*

am ....

pm..

If you have the chance to travel, you should grab it with both hands and you can make great gains through the involvement of friends in your life. All in all, this should be a very positive period. You still have it in mind to treat yourself in some way and the lure of luxury is very strong.

28 SUNDAY *Moon Age Day 13 Moon Sign Aries*

am ....

pm..

Although some jobs might take you longer than you anticipate, the Capricorn need to do things properly is in evidence. Friends should be both warm and supportive. Seeking out a variety of interests could be fun this weekend and would certainly be better than sitting around and waiting for life to come to you.

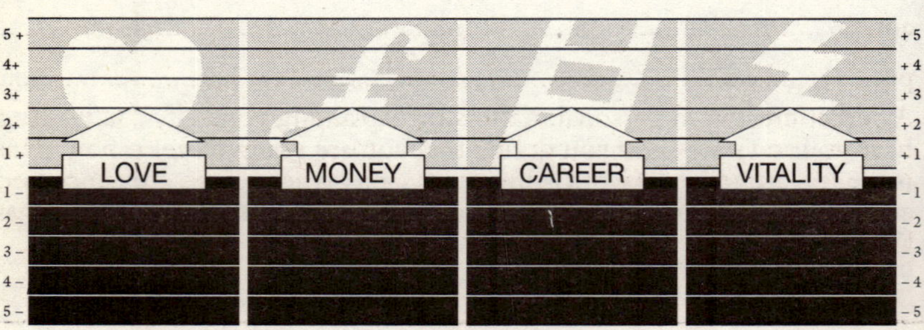

29 MONDAY *Moon Age Day 14 Moon Sign Aries*

am ....

pm ....

Routines are easy to deal with, though you would rather be having a good time, probably in the company of people you find interesting and stimulating. The everyday world can seem just a little tedious now. Trends suggest that there may be a significant improvement in relationships at the beginning of this week.

30 TUESDAY *Moon Age Day 15 Moon Sign Taurus*

am ....

pm ....

It's time to show someone how much you care, so go to town and make the best of impressions. Having a ball on the way would be fun so you could be celebrating well into the evening. The focus is on your love life and on romance today, with more than one planet lining up to offer you interesting opportunities.

31 WEDNESDAY *Moon Age Day 16 Moon Sign Taurus*

am ....

pm ....

A breath of fresh air would probably do you good today and would blow away a few accumulated cobwebs. Confidence grows as the day gets older. This would be a good time to find ingenious solutions to existing problems and to solve a mystery that has been bugging you for some time.

1 THURSDAY *Moon Age Day 17 Moon Sign Gemini*

am ....

pm ....

A deeply creative streak, which runs through all Capricorns, is beginning to show itself now. This means you may not be giving quite as much time to the practicalities of life as you should, but you are a hard worker and can certainly catch up later. Rules and regulations can be the bane of your life around now, so steer clear of them if you can.

2 FRIDAY *Moon Age Day 18 Moon Sign Gemini*

am..

pm..

For the moment, you will be happy to watch life go by and less inclined than of late to look for riotous social company. Part of your nature is actually very nostalgic around now. There isn't a great deal of dynamic ambition and drive today, but this is only a very short-term trend and due to end almost immediately.

3 SATURDAY *Moon Age Day 19 Moon Sign Gemini*

am..

pm..

You might not see very much of family members today because you are likely to be so busy. Nevertheless, the most powerful focus right now is upon close personal attachments, but that doesn't mean you are ignoring the world at large. On the contrary, you virtually demand to be out there in the middle of whatever is happening.

4 SUNDAY *Moon Age Day 20 Moon Sign Cancer*

am..

pm..

Instead of offering support, you now find yourself receiving it. Potentially speaking, the arrival of the lunar low can take the wind out of your sails. If you are prepared, the situation will not be half as bad as it could be. There are confidences to keep, and although practical matters are on the back burner, love and attention is very noticeable.

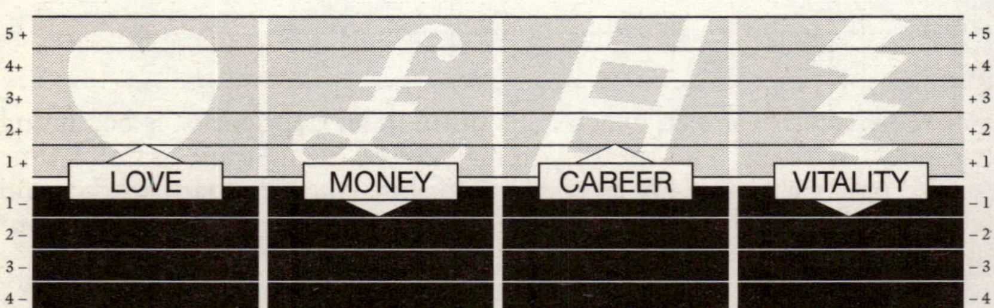

November 2012

Your Month at a Glance

⊕ = Opportunities are around ⊖ = Be on the defensive ● = Life is pretty ordinary

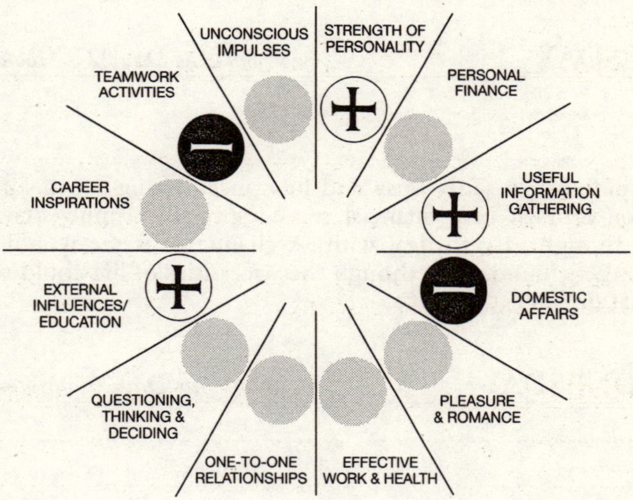

November Highs and Lows

Here I show you how the rhythms of the Moon will affect you this month. Like the tide, your energies and abilities will rise and fall with its pattern. When it is above the centre line, go for it, when it is below, you should be resting.

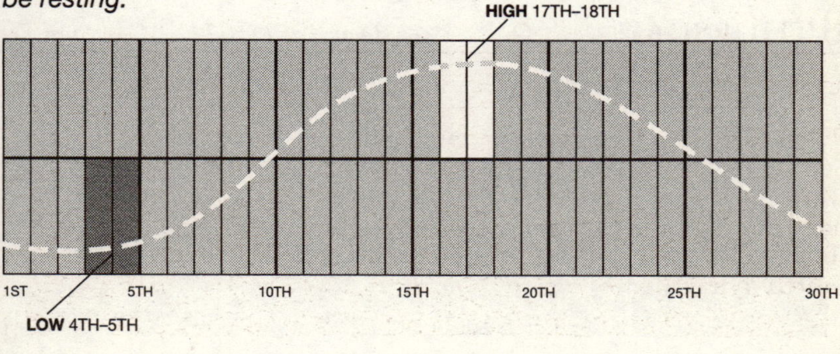

5 MONDAY *Moon Age Day 21 Moon Sign Cancer*

am ....

pm..

Get on side with those who have ideas that broadly parallel your own and don't be afraid to take a few calculated risks. Though you feel generally that you are less in control of your own life in some ways than usual, as long as you are willing to co-operate with others, this should not really prove to be a particular issue.

6 TUESDAY *Moon Age Day 22 Moon Sign Leo*

am ....

pm..

You should remain fairly busy and be concentrating on making things better for yourself in a financial sense especially. Family demands are present, though easy to deal with. A change of scene would suit you down to the ground, even though the necessities of life could make that somewhat difficult to achieve.

7 WEDNESDAY ☿ *Moon Age Day 23 Moon Sign Leo*

am ....

pm..

It is likely that you are not looking at things quite as logically as would normally be the case and emotions can get in your way. Most important is to keep a smile on your face, even when you feel jumpy. Someone might be trying to put you down in the minds of others, or at least that's how it will appear to you right now.

8 THURSDAY ☿ *Moon Age Day 24 Moon Sign Leo*

am ....

pm..

Staying in one place could prove to be something of a bind, particularly when movement looks so potentially interesting and rewarding. This is not a day during which you can afford to take anything for granted. You should check and double-check all details, especially if any of them are related to travel.

9 FRIDAY ☿ *Moon Age Day 25 Moon Sign Virgo*

am ....

pm ....

This is a good time to get rid of dead wood and to consign redundant ideas to the dustbin of life. It's very late in the year to think about spring cleaning, but in a way that is what you are doing today. Do be slightly careful though because for Capricorn this could lead to a sense of insecurity.

10 SATURDAY ☿ *Moon Age Day 26 Moon Sign Virgo*

am ....

pm ....

Courage is necessary in public situations but you should come good in sporting activities. A much more settled period comes along as far as your personal life is concerned. Don't be too quick to offer advice, because you could find yourself refusing the same suggestions yourself before very long.

11 SUNDAY ☿ *Moon Age Day 27 Moon Sign Libra*

am ....

pm ....

Single Capricorns should be looking for new relationships around now and all sorts of people tend to make offers that are difficult to refuse. Practical matters are important but emotions rule the roost. Take advantage of some quality time that comes along today and spend precious moments with someone you really care for.

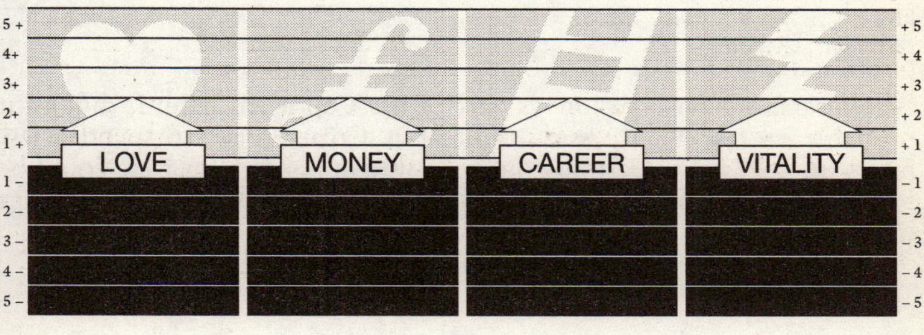

12 MONDAY ☿ *Moon Age Day 28 Moon Sign Libra*

am ....

pm ....

Things could be slightly sluggish in a professional sense, so it would be best to do only what you have to at work. Domestically speaking, life should be rather easier to address and, in truth, you will be happiest today when at home. You might relish the prospect of simply putting your feet up.

13 TUESDAY ☿ *Moon Age Day 0 Moon Sign Scorpio*

am ....

pm ....

Keep a sense of proportion when dealing with issues that have stumped you in the past. Persistence pays off in the end. Friends could turn out to be quite helpful, often in fairly unexpected ways. Don't be too proud to accept their proffered assistance, even though in at least some cases you could manage better on your own.

14 WEDNESDAY ☿ *Moon Age Day 1 Moon Sign Scorpio*

am ....

pm ....

A generally lucrative period continues, though you won't have everything you would wish today. Part of the reason for this is that some of your expectations are not entirely realistic. This only leads to disappointments if you fail to realise how life really is. A more contemplative phase is needed.

15 THURSDAY ☿ *Moon Age Day 2 Moon Sign Sagittarius*

am ....

pm ....

Being paranoid on occasions is part of the Capricorn nature, though it probably isn't at all necessary right now. Create space to spend a few hours on your own. Getting your own way in financial matters could be surprisingly easy, probably leading you to being rather suspicious about others.

16 FRIDAY ☿ *Moon Age Day 3 Moon Sign Sagittarius*

am ....

pm ....

The end of the working week makes specific demands of you, and especially so in a work sense. You may be quite pleased to lay down some responsibilities by the evening. Trends assist your mind to work swiftly, leading you to arrive at some quite staggering conclusions, often on the spur of the moment.

17 SATURDAY ☿ *Moon Age Day 4 Moon Sign Capricorn*

am ....

pm ....

This is a potentially good day and a time during which you can make the most of just about any opportunity that comes your way. Creatively speaking, you know what looks and feels right and you can gain support from some unexpected directions. You could surprise yourself with your boldness right now.

18 SUNDAY ☿ *Moon Age Day 5 Moon Sign Capricorn*

am ....

pm ....

With the lunar high comes a sudden burst of enthusiasm and energy. It's as if you have a rocket strapped to your back, so getting through any number of jobs should be a piece of cake! This would be an ideal time to take a journey, preferably in the enjoyable company of your partner or a good friend.

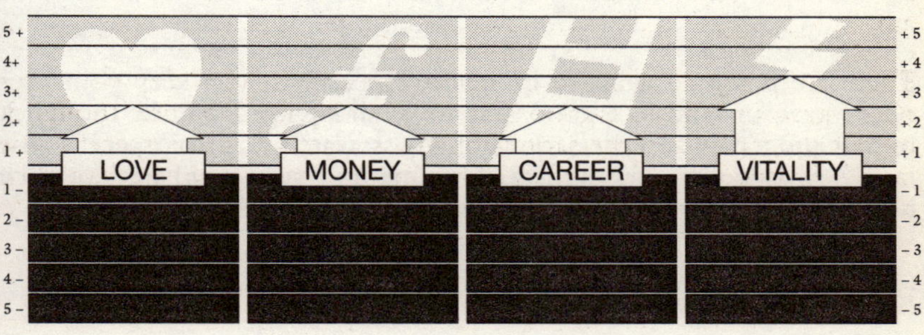

19 MONDAY ☿ *Moon Age Day 6 Moon Sign Aquarius*

am ....

pm ....

There is tremendous scope for advancement at work, plus extra incentive to go out and get what you want. Although you will come across obstacles at some stage during the day, these are unlikely to hold you back. You still feel good about yourself and life in general as the week gets started.

20 TUESDAY ☿ *Moon Age Day 7 Moon Sign Aquarius*

am ....

pm ....

All of a sudden you are struck by a burning need for luxuries of one sort or another. Capricorn is quite insecure and owning new things feeds your self-esteem. Of course, lots of material possessions aren't really necessary but as long as you don't break the family bank, you can probably afford to indulge yourself a little.

21 WEDNESDAY ☿ *Moon Age Day 8 Moon Sign Pisces*

am ....

pm ....

It's the simpler things in life that appeal most at present, for example the company of good friends and being able to enjoy a well-cooked meal. Social trends are good. It is easier to get what you want from life now, but typical of your nature, you probably won't want it any more.

22 THURSDAY ☿ *Moon Age Day 9 Moon Sign Pisces*

am ....

pm ....

There are potential gains to be made, especially if you keep your eyes open, so this would be a good time to go shopping. Don't be too quick to pass judgement on the actions of an associate or acquaintance. Close family encounters work well at this time and you could find yourself heavily involved in plans for Christmas.

23 FRIDAY ☿ *Moon Age Day 10 Moon Sign Pisces*

am ....

pm..

Seek out the advice and maybe the help of people who are experts in their respective fields. Even Capricorn cannot do everything for itself. The speed of life increases and it is obvious that you are trying to keep up with matters that are beyond your capability to control.

24 SATURDAY ☿ *Moon Age Day 11 Moon Sign Aries*

am ....

pm..

Some confusion in your social life could arise, as you try to do a dozen different things at the same time. There could also be some surprising and very interesting news later in the day. Look out for a period of probable professional gain, mainly brought about as a result of your own attitude and hard work.

25 SUNDAY ☿ *Moon Age Day 12 Moon Sign Aries*

am ....

pm..

Around this time you can expect a number of surprises and unbidden events, all of which contribute to a general increase in interest and participation on your part. The planets suggest that the domestic atmosphere is likely to become livelier, with much communication and a possible visit from relatives or friends.

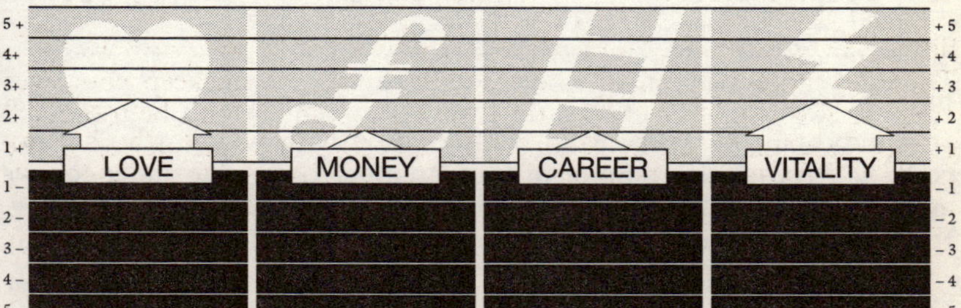

26 MONDAY ☿ *Moon Age Day 13 Moon Sign Taurus*

am ....

pm...

There are gains to be made in a financial sense, with people from the past paying renewed visits to your life. You might feel strangely calm and serene later in the day. Though today is likely to be hectic from a social point of view, you are certainly kept in touch with everything that is going on in your vicinity.

27 TUESDAY ☿ *Moon Age Day 14 Moon Sign Taurus*

am ....

pm...

This is not a time to speculate more than necessary and you would definitely be sensible to put a temporary curb on any big spending. Avoid too much optimism where money is concerned. Sorting out a mess that someone else has created could take up a small part of your day, though the effort should be worthwhile.

28 WEDNESDAY *Moon Age Day 15 Moon Sign Taurus*

am ....

pm...

Family concerns that are somehow related to plans for Christmas are not likely to hold you up for long because you are able to think up new strategies on the hoof. You may be anxious to get on with plans for the future, but there are some restrictions around at present that will confuse you somewhat.

29 THURSDAY *Moon Age Day 16 Moon Sign Gemini*

am ....

pm...

It is important today to avoid confrontation with people who are not really worth your effort. Some of your attempts to keep life under control are going wrong. The results are likely to be more amusing than annoying, though there could be times today when the odd frustration will creep in.

30 FRIDAY *Moon Age Day 17 Moon Sign Gemini*

am ....

pm ....

Talk to people and truly listen to what they have to say. Compromise is necessary and that isn't a particularly tall order for the presently easy-going zodiac sign of Capricorn. Although there is little in the way of harmony in your relationships today, part of the reason could be frustrations you find difficult to address.

1 SATURDAY *Moon Age Day 18 Moon Sign Cancer*

am ....

pm ....

A few obstacles could prevent you from making quite as much of today as you would wish. However, if you set your stall out carefully, you should be able to get away with barely noticing the lunar low. This would not be a good day to climb a mountain or to take part in other vigorous exercise.

2 SUNDAY *Moon Age Day 19 Moon Sign Cancer*

am ....

pm ....

Stick to the simple things of life and spend some time spoiling yourself. There is an active and very demanding period ahead, so it won't do you any harm to charge up those batteries. Confidence isn't really dented, unless you come face to face with people who seem determined to put you down.

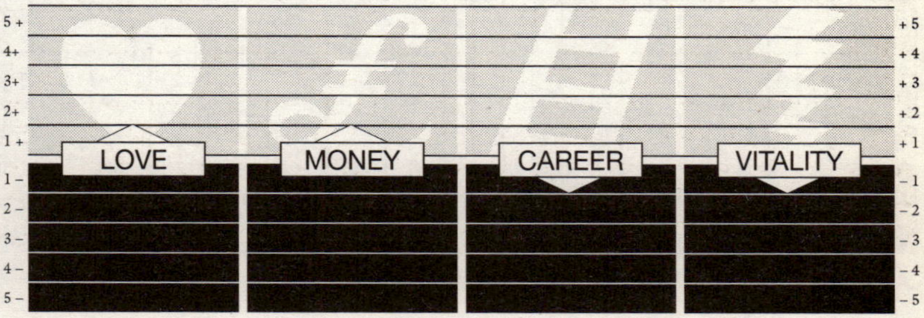

December 2012

Your Month at a Glance

(+) = Opportunities are around   (–) = Be on the defensive   (●) = Life is pretty ordinary

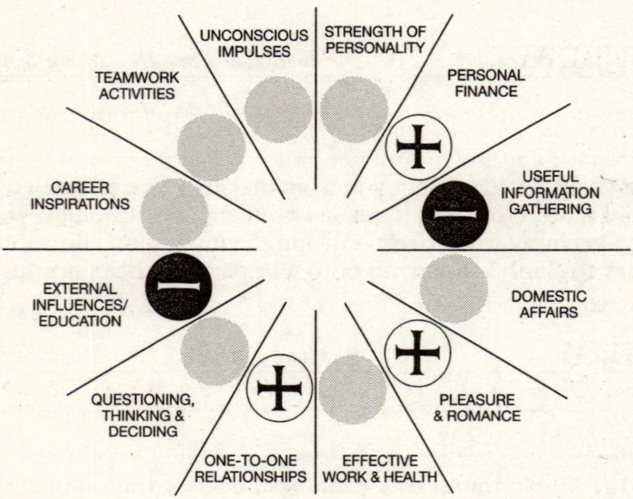

December Highs and Lows

Here I show you how the rhythms of the Moon will affect you this month. Like the tide, your energies and abilities will rise and fall with its pattern. When it is above the centre line, go for it, when it is below, you should be resting.

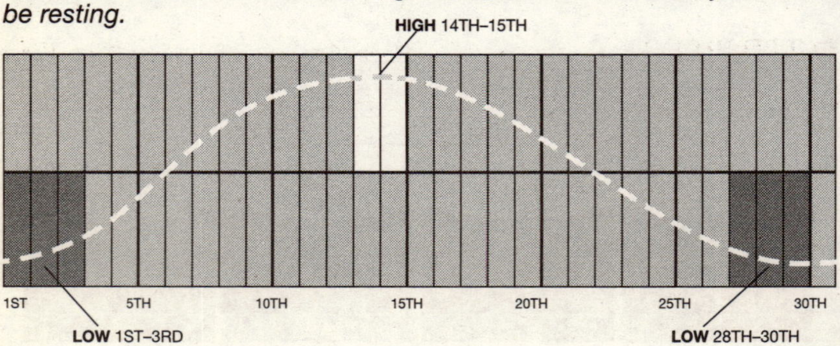

3 MONDAY *Moon Age Day 20 Moon Sign Cancer*

am ....

pm ....

With one eye on Christmas and the other on what you want to achieve materially, there isn't a great deal of time to spare right now. Don't overbook yourself for next weekend. It's not that long until Christmas and there may be shopping you have forgotten. Get ready to make tracks and get ahead professionally.

4 TUESDAY *Moon Age Day 21 Moon Sign Leo*

am ....

pm ....

It may dawn on you today that Christmas is quite close, leaving you less time than you thought to get everything done the way you would wish. You may need a little mental refreshment at any time now. That means ringing the changes and mixing with people who are not normally part of your circle.

5 WEDNESDAY *Moon Age Day 22 Moon Sign Leo*

am ....

pm ....

Don't be very surprised if nostalgic associations take over at some stage during the day, particularly if you have children. There are almost certainly some surprises on the social scene, together with a desire to get on well with people generally. Because you are a Capricorn, it is likely that you have everything prepared for your social life.

6 THURSDAY *Moon Age Day 23 Moon Sign Virgo*

am ....

pm ....

Compliments are easy to come by and you are likely to turn heads wherever you go, especially by the evening. Though career aims might have rather less going for them than has been the case lately, you should certainly be enjoying yourself in terms of your personal life.

7 FRIDAY *Moon Age Day 24 Moon Sign Virgo*

am..

pm..

You will be quite busy in a moment by moment sense, but you need to save time to show your lover how much you care. The response you get is very positive and should see you finishing the day on a high note. Personal and intimate matters are the most rewarding of all today.

8 SATURDAY *Moon Age Day 25 Moon Sign Libra*

am..

pm..

It looks as though it is time to get your party hat on. Although Christmas is still some time away, you are in the mood to boogie. Perhaps what you are doing today has little or nothing to do with the festive season but you do need to let your hair down. Don't be held back by pointless and stupid conventions at this time.

9 SUNDAY *Moon Age Day 26 Moon Sign Libra*

am..

pm..

Get out and about if you can, though it is likely that your main destination will be the local shopping centre. Getting along with others isn't too difficult this weekend, just as long as they are willing to do more or less exactly what you ask. The fact is that you are being rather more selfish than would normally be the case.

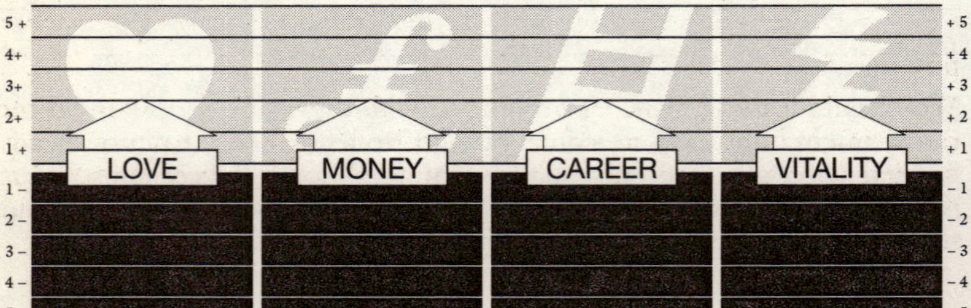

10 MONDAY *Moon Age Day 27 Moon Sign Scorpio*

am ....

pm ....

Today it's a case of 'speak the truth and shame the devil', which is fine as long as you remember to use a little Capricorn tact on the way. You could get the feeling that you are speaking out of turn today. That's okay, because unless you say what you think, how on earth will others know?

11 TUESDAY *Moon Age Day 28 Moon Sign Scorpio*

am ....

pm ....

Although today starts out fairly steadily, things should soon heat up. Progress is hard to see at first, which is why by lunch time you have to put in that extra bit of effort that can make all the difference. By the evening, you can be the life and soul of any party. If there isn't one on offer, you might create a shindig yourself.

12 WEDNESDAY *Moon Age Day 0 Moon Sign Sagittarius*

am ....

pm ....

Offer others a helping hand in specific tasks that are familiar to you but don't get in the way if younger people are seeking independence. A sense that you can rely only on yourself might prevail today. Up to a point that might be the case, but you ought to give friends the benefit of the doubt all the same.

13 THURSDAY *Moon Age Day 1 Moon Sign Sagittarius*

am ....

pm ....

You should learn to trust, as others are willing to trust you. Only in the rarest of circumstances are you likely to be let down. Beware a heavy-handed approach at home, particularly with younger people, who are only seeking to spread their wings. Confidence to do the right thing is there, but you need to look for it.

14 FRIDAY *Moon Age Day 2 Moon Sign Capricorn*

am ....

pm ....

Energy levels remain very high and you can certainly set out to make this day your own in a number of different ways. If things are not fast enough for you, then step up the pace yourself. Despite being extremely active, you should make time to show genuine compassion to someone in your immediate vicinity.

15 SATURDAY *Moon Age Day 3 Moon Sign Capricorn*

am ....

pm ....

All in all, this could be one of the best days of December for shopping. Financially speaking, there could be some minor improvements now, and not a moment too soon with Christmas so close. Nevertheless, you need to spend wisely and make sure to look out for those bargains that lie around every corner.

16 SUNDAY *Moon Age Day 4 Moon Sign Aquarius*

am ....

pm ....

It isn't often that Capricorn is duped and once you realise that this is a possibility today, you will be on your guard. Look for the humour in family relationships and interaction. Avoid potentially deceptive situations if at all possible this Sunday. If you are about to sign a document, read the small print very carefully.

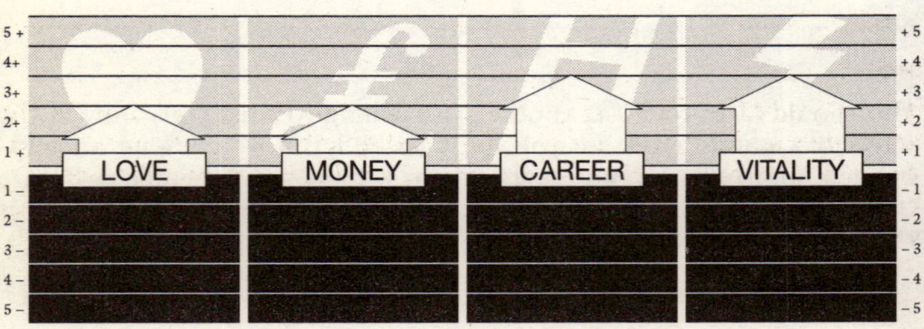

17 MONDAY *Moon Age Day 5 Moon Sign Aquarius*

am ....

pm ....

It isn't difficult for you to maintain a high profile in most situations at the start of this working week. Many Capricorns will be putting thoughts of Christmas on hold, opting instead for the chance to get ahead in a professional sense. Be aware that people really do what to hear what you are saying at present.

18 TUESDAY *Moon Age Day 6 Moon Sign Aquarius*

am ....

pm ....

You ought to be in fine spirits and very willing to have a go at more or less anything. Stay away from contentious topics of conversation because you are apt to speak your mind around now. This is very much a go-ahead period and one which offers you the vitality to get everything right ahead of the holidays.

19 WEDNESDAY *Moon Age Day 7 Moon Sign Pisces*

am ....

pm ....

Your way of dealing with disputes that arise in your vicinity today could seem somehow inappropriate when seen from the perspective of others. If at all possible you should give people the benefit of the doubt, since there is a good chance you are being told the absolute truth as they see it.

20 THURSDAY *Moon Age Day 8 Moon Sign Pisces*

am ....

pm ....

This is a very fruitful period with regard to furthering career aims. There are people around who seem willing and able to lend a helping hand, whilst at the same time you ought to find specific family members coping rather better than of late. Quell a burning desire to make radical changes so close to Christmas.

21 FRIDAY *Moon Age Day 9 Moon Sign Aries*

am ....

pm...

You might feel that your partner, or maybe a family member, is being rather bossier than you are willing to accept. Remember the time of year and bite your tongue. When you finally get around to understanding what the irritation actually is, you should be glad that you managed to keep your cool.

22 SATURDAY *Moon Age Day 10 Moon Sign Aries*

am ....

pm...

Rewards come along as a result of decisions and actions you took in the past, maybe bringing better financial wherewithal. Your personal magnetism is beginning to show and with Christmas only a couple of days away you are able to create a positively magical setting, particularly for younger people.

23 SUNDAY *Moon Age Day 11 Moon Sign Taurus*

am ....

pm...

Your powers of attraction are strong and there are few people who remain immune to your charms. As a result, this is the best time of all to go out and get what you want. On this, the last weekend before Christmas, you may want to finalise certain details; that is if your family will leave you enough time to do so.

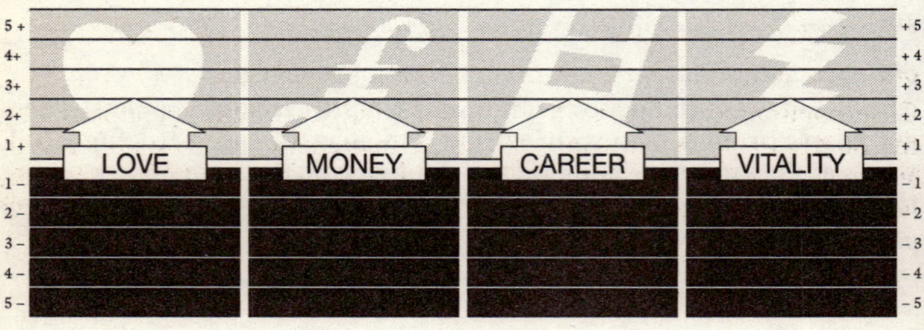

24 MONDAY *Moon Age Day 12 Moon Sign Taurus*

am ....

pm ....

You could easily find that you are occupying a centre-stage position right now and would be willing to entertain others. This might not be what Capricorn is about as a rule but you do have it within you now to be extremely showy. At heart, you are still as keen to look after your own life and circumstances as is always the case.

25 TUESDAY *Moon Age Day 13 Moon Sign Taurus*

am ....

pm ....

You receive significant emotional support and return it in kind. Not surprisingly, family associations are well accented right now. A lovely mix of planetary trends surrounds you during Christmas Day. Some of them are quiet, so you may not choose to be socially active all the time.

26 WEDNESDAY *Moon Age Day 14 Moon Sign Gemini*

am ....

pm ....

You might have to sacrifice your own interests a little this Boxing Day, in favour of thinking about the group. This might be family or it could be your friends but there is no doubt that you are very generous in your feelings and actions now. There are contrasts around you, not least of all in the way others behave.

27 THURSDAY *Moon Age Day 15 Moon Sign Gemini*

am ....

pm ....

Clear communication is the key and can avoid you being disappointed by the outcome of any encounter. Business matters are now variable but in any case you might have other things on your mind. Avoid others getting hold of the wrong end of the stick by being willing to explain yourself properly early in the day.

28 FRIDAY *Moon Age Day 16 Moon Sign Cancer*

am ....

pm..

Remaining in one place, though restful, will not stimulate certain aspects of your nature at this time. This is a good day for visiting family members and friends at a distance, or for treating yourself in some way. Finances could be stronger than you expected.

29 SATURDAY *Moon Age Day 17 Moon Sign Cancer*

am ....

pm..

The lunar low makes its presence felt but you don't have to allow that to prevent you from having fun. As long as you allow others to make the arrangements, and the running, you can sit back and enjoy yourself.

30 SUNDAY *Moon Age Day 18 Moon Sign Cancer*

am ....

pm..

Today you are able to ignore people you don't like very much, rather than reacting adversely to them. Routines can be tedious right now and if this proves to be the case, find ways to sidestep them.

31 MONDAY *Moon Age Day 19 Moon Sign Leo*

am ....

pm..

Resolutions made today are likely to be as a result of a great deal of thought earlier in the year. It appears that this is a particularly good phase for any sort of intimacy between yourself and your partner.

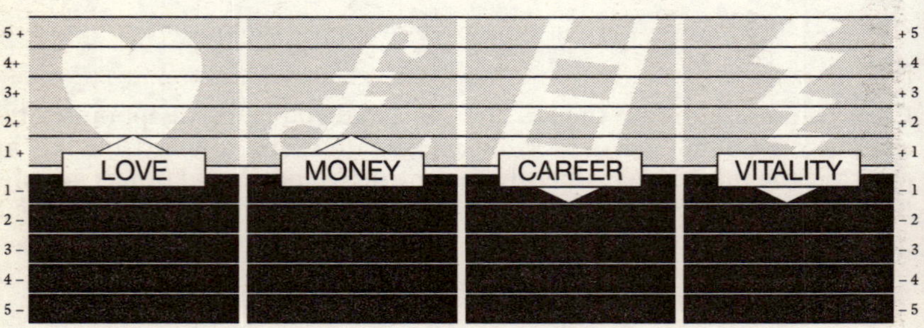

RISING SIGNS FOR CAPRICORN

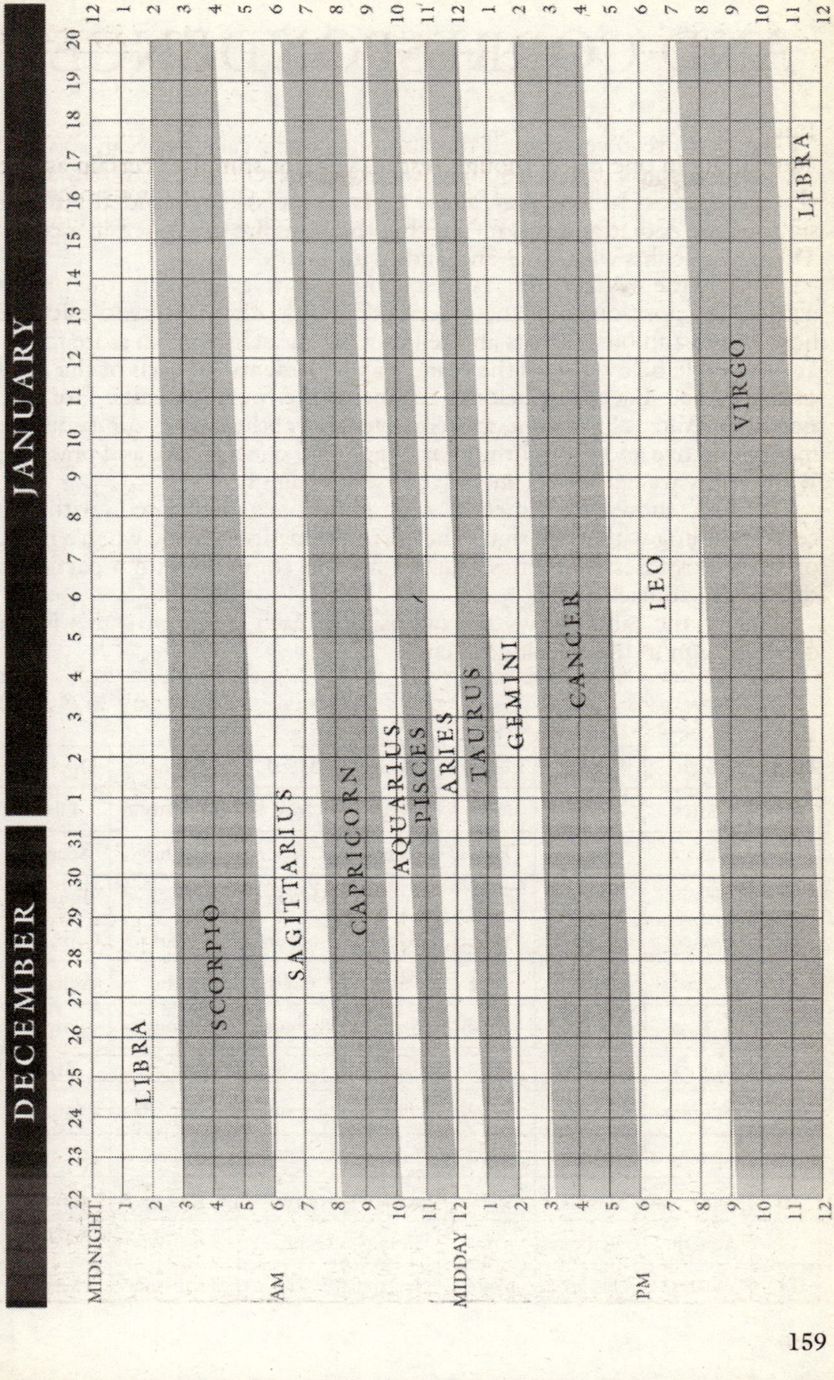

THE ZODIAC, PLANETS AND CORRESPONDENCES

The Earth revolves around the Sun once every calendar year, so when viewed from Earth the Sun appears in a different part of the sky as the year progresses. In astrology, these parts of the sky are divided into the signs of the zodiac and this means that the signs are organised in a circle. The circle begins with Aries and ends with Pisces.

Taking the zodiac sign as a starting point, astrologers then work with all the positions of planets, stars and many other factors to calculate horoscopes and birth charts and tell us what the stars have in store for us.

The table below shows the planets and Elements for each of the signs of the zodiac. Each sign belongs to one of the four Elements: Fire, Air, Earth or Water. Fire signs are creative and enthusiastic; Air signs are mentally active and thoughtful; Earth signs are constructive and practical; Water signs are emotional and have strong feelings.

It also shows the metals and gemstones associated with, or corresponding with, each sign. The correspondence is made when a metal or stone possesses properties that are held in common with a particular sign of the zodiac.

Finally, the table shows the opposite of each star sign – this is the opposite sign in the astrological circle.

Placed	Sign	Symbol	Element	Planet	Metal	Stone	Opposite
1	Aries	Ram	Fire	Mars	Iron	Bloodstone	Libra
2	Taurus	Bull	Earth	Venus	Copper	Sapphire	Scorpio
3	Gemini	Twins	Air	Mercury	Mercury	Tiger's Eye	Sagittarius
4	Cancer	Crab	Water	Moon	Silver	Pearl	Capricorn
5	Leo	Lion	Fire	Sun	Gold	Ruby	Aquarius
6	Virgo	Maiden	Earth	Mercury	Mercury	Sardonyx	Pisces
7	Libra	Scales	Air	Venus	Copper	Sapphire	Aries
8	Scorpio	Scorpion	Water	Pluto	Plutonium	Jasper	Taurus
9	Sagittarius	Archer	Fire	Jupiter	Tin	Topaz	Gemini
10	Capricorn	Goat	Earth	Saturn	Lead	Black Onyx	Cancer
11	Aquarius	Waterbearer	Air	Uranus	Uranium	Amethyst	Leo
12	Pisces	Fishes	Water	Neptune	Tin	Moonstone	Virgo